IT COULD HAVE BEEN ME

Overcoming Life's Challenges

DR. JEFFREY MOORE

Printed in the United States of America

ISBN: Softcover   979-8-88622-430-6
           eBook   979-8-88622-431-3
Republished by: PageTurner Press and Media LLC
Publication Date: 07/12/2022

To order copies of this book, contact:
PageTurner Press and Media
Phone: 1-888-447-9651
info@pageturner.us
www.pageturner.us

TABLE OF CONTENTS

DEDICATION

With this being my first attempt as an author, there are so many to whom I could quite easily and humbly dedicate this book. Above all, this book is a direct reflection of my personal spiritual and creative connection with God through Jesus Christ.

This writing is dedicated with greatest love and in remembrance of my dearly departed grandmother Anliza Moore, whose exemplary walk as a strong Christian woman and family matriarch shaped my course in life to be the best I can be through Christ Jesus. We miss you down here but delight in our family reunion that will take place in Heaven.

And to my little brother Brian Torin Moore, whose life was taken from us by complications associated with COVID-19 during the Pandemic, before the vaccinations. I miss you "Underdog"! He may have considered me his hero, but he will forever be mine! Rest in Heaven!

Forever and always, I dedicate this writing to my loving children – Cheryl (James), Lovar (Tawanda), Christopher (Sara), Katrina and Karla; as well as my twelve grandchildren.

I have for years and will continue to save the best acknowledgement for last - my biggest supporter and help mate, my wife - Mary.

ACKNOWLEDGMENTS

As I repeatedly thank God for pouring diligence, patience, and knowledge into me daily, I can't help to let it be known that it was He who afforded me the opportunity and the perseverance to complete this milestone achievement in my life.

As Pastor of a church which has for 25 years touched the lives of hundreds of people, especially mine in ways that add and shape character. The biggest bonus that God delivers to the church through its Pastor is the thrill of witnessing the changing of lives changed right before your eyes.

I must thank my entire church family - past and present - at New Birth Church (formerly Greater Antioch Baptist Church), located in Oceanside, California, North San Diego area, and partnering ministries who have prayerfully supported their Bishop during these many years of ministry and laboring. It is a joy and I count it a privilege to serve one of the finest young and upcoming churches in the Lord's vineyard. Truly, they exemplify the theme of the church "being doers of the Word, and not just hearers". Then further separating themselves from the ordinary church environment which has chased so many away by standing on a promise lifted from the scriptures found in Jeremiah 31:3, "With love and kindness, He has drawn us." Each person representing the whole team unity of this body unsacrificially giving their all. To this, we are now an international outreach touching lives across the globe and living obediently to fulfill the Great Commission given by our Lord Jesus. Additionally, God's blessings to the many visitors, former members, friends and supporters of this great church and its pastor. We pray that our encounters past, present, and future have been and will be crafted in the spirit of love and God receives the highest honors and glory.

First, I give all praise and honor to my Lord Jesus Christ, who is the Head of my life. He is my greatest inspiration and motivation. Special thanks to my family, friends and co-laborers for your love and support throughout the years. I never could have done any of this without you!In precious memory of the late pastors - the Rev. Dr. Lawrence Edwards (Uncle Jack), the Rev. W. W. Wright, the Rev. Dr. Willie James Smith, Justice Thomas Hammonds, the Rev. Dr. Timothy Winters, the Rev. Dr. Thomas W. Davis, and the Honorable Bishop Dr. George Dallas McKinney.

Also, to other great leaders who have inspired me tremendously— the Rev. Don Conley, the Rev. Dr. Charles Lundy, the Rev. Dr. Booker T. Crenshaw, Bishop Derrick Robinson, and Superintendent James Gaines. Without their input and sources of knowledge, I would not be as adequately equipped for ministry as I am today.

Thank you all once again, especially Page Turner Press & Media for recapturing my creative works through this revised edition. May God continue to bless you as He has done me and my house, and I will continue to "Hold to God's Unchanging Hand!"

ENDORSEMENT

Bishop Jeffrey Moore,

Congratulations for your obedience in writing this book. I was informed and inspired by the book's content. The Holy Spirit has planted many insights and truths that you have delivered. Thank you for your book.

God bless you always!

Your friend and brother,

Bishop George D. McKinney

St. Stephens Church of God in Christ

August 17, 2019

INTRODUCTION

You Don't Know My Story

Sometimes you wonder how you ever can attain success in life realizing that you started off from the bottom of life's ladder. Coming from where I'm from? Or so they say! Why do so many people wrongfully judge the book by the cover, without knowing in depth, the content and character. Face value, genetics, heritage or where you came from can or should be determining factors of how far you're going! Well, I guess you would say one rung at a time. Calculated steps that one finds themselves working to progress forward. The issue arises out of a thing called determination. Okay, if you add motivation and an occasional push from someone whose advice means alot to your moving in the right direction matters much.

What do you do when the spoon is not silver or if it was supposed to be but got tarnished along the way? At least, you may say most successful people came from hopeful positions, career-oriented parents, nice homes, and no worries - sounds too much like the Huxtables. Coming from where I came from meant no Heathcliff in the house, one working Mom and believe me, not a lawyer like

Claire. Well, at least there was a roof.

As a child, did you ever dream big just to establish somewhere to place your mind to guide your hopes. I don't get me wrong, everyone starts somewhere, why not from a place of you'll never go, be or do anything to look at far the Lord has brought me. Sometimes dreams need to be spawn from meager beginnings for you to know and realize that not by my will, but by the Will of God who has the power to guide our steps.

any scenes in life have been etched and engraved permanently into our minds upon a space called memory. Some are just as vivid and clear today as they were at the time they occurred. Memories have a way of allowing us to take a stroll backward in time to recall both the good and the bad; although, we tend to suppress the trials and tribulations and instead constantly replay and celebrate the best of times.

Isn't it amazing how God has created the brain as a master storage unit that, at will, can hit the rewind button and replay scenes that have helped shape the kind of people we have become! In some cases, those flashbacks put you in certain places, conditions, and opportunities in which you can look back with astonishment and think, "*It could have been me!*"

If you consider this for a moment, it seems that often, God's people, even those who proclaim already to be Christians, are faced with a great deal of pressure distracting them from the course that God has already predestined for their lives. God has predetermined the path of His people even amid rising problems and concerns in our society and even with the measurable waning of faith among the people of God. God is still committed to helping us obtain the best

He has to offer. The real challenge lies within us and our ability to mature or "grow up in all things into Him who is the head."

The Bible puts it this way: "that we should no longer be children, tossed to and fro and carried about with every wind of doctrine, by the trickery of men, in the cunning craftiness of deceitful plotting, but, speaking the truth in love, may grow up in all things into Him who is the head—Christ" (Ephesians 4:14–15).

Crowds of people go to movies to see stories portrayed on the big screen. People read books filled with great stories either in paper form or electronic. Stories have been illustrated in many forms, but those stories that really paint a vivid, captivating picture are the ones to catch our attention. I want you to step into this frame personally and picture this: It could have been me—in a wheelchair with no one to help me get where I need to go. It could have been me—being homeless, struggling to find food, clothing, and shelter. It could have been me—struggling with teenage pregnancy or selling my body just to live. It could have been me—the object of abuse and mental trauma. If this strikes a chord in you, then you're like many today, but if not, how about this? It could have been me—strung out on crack cocaine, weed, or crystal meth; popping too many pills; drowning my life in a bottle of booze; or sitting behind bars with two strikes facing life for a thoughtless mistake. Possibly, any one of these could have been you or me, but for the grace of God, they aren't. Let me invite you to continue reading, and maybe you'll come to a similar conclusion.

As we set forth to develop the final scene, what will our lives play out to be when run from start to finish? And then each of us must think to ourselves, *How will I finish?* Do this with me: Take a look back over your life, and replay the various scenes, whether good or bad, joyful or sorrowful. Reverse to the moment you sprang forth as a newborn babe and move to your present and dare to ponder your future. How will you finish? Well, as God takes His seat in the director's chair of our lives… lights, camera, action! Is this your story?

CHAPTER 1

Rick's Story: I Can't Help Myself

Hear my cry, O God; listen to my prayer. From the ends
of the earth I call to you, I call as my heart grows faint;
lead me to the rock that is higher than I. For you have
been my refuge, a strong tower against the foe. I long to
dwell in your tent forever and take refuge in the shelter
of your wings.

—Psalm 61:1–4 NIV

The Nowhere Man

It was December 1965 when one of the greatest musical groups of
all time, the Beatles, released the album *Rubber Soul* and sang out their
philosophy on humankind with compelling power for my generation.
Perhaps my story is clearly illustrated in the first two lines from John
Lennon's song "Nowhere Man": "He's a real nowhere man / Sitting in
his nowhere land."

Who would have ever thought *that I would end up like this... a real nowhere man? No reason to live any longer. Just look at me: Richard "Rick" Bosley. A highly decorated Vietnam War veteran and hero. America's finest and one of the few who made it out of my little country town in the hills of Pennsylvania. Look at me. I've become a broken shell of a man.*

Depressive thoughts and feelings of uselessness overwhelmed me. Looking up at a paint-chipped ceiling, I shouted, "Who can I protect now when I can't even help myself?"

I sat there, day in and day out, staring at the walls of my empty room…desolate, lifeless, and lonely. It was a room filled with so many memories that utterly haunted me, a room that had been like a prison to me, a man who had done so much to make our nation free and secure for all. The room had seemed so large when I was growing up, but now it seemed hardly large enough for me to move around. It seemed to be closing in on me by the minute.

Why had life dished me such a rotten egg? Why me? Why, after all I had done and tried to do for my country? I peered endlessly at the drab four corners and asked myself, "Why was I dealt such an awful hand?" Kenny Rogers wrote a song about a gambler, and as I sat there, I thought about the words to that song. *Do you suppose that was me, and now I'm awakening from my dream world to face reality?* I had gambled away the good fortunes of my life to come to this point of decision with tiny voices in my head telling me to "hold 'em or fold 'em."

Son of a Coal Miner

I was born in Pennsylvania, the third of five children. I had two older sisters and two younger brothers. Although we lived in a small wooden shack on land owned by someone else, we were able to raise the usual crops, such as corn, tomatoes, and snap peas. We even had some chickens, pigs, and a cow named Bessie for milking.

Our family was poor, and Pa worked in the coal mines near Scranton so we would have money to eat and make do. Ma stayed at home and mostly minded us kids, with the occasional job of doing other folks' laundry. We kids would go to school and then do our chores in the afternoon before we did our homework for class the next day.

Ma placed my sisters in charge of us. We did everything we were supposed to do and maybe got some playtime in before we came in for the night. I didn't like my sisters always telling us what to do. Every now and then I would say, "You're not the boss of me," and Loretta, the oldest, would tell me, "Ma put me in charge, and that *does* make me the boss of you, and if you don't mind me, I'm gonna tell Ma." We all knew what would happen if she told Ma, so we acted right. I must admit, though, that my two little brothers and I gave our sisters all that they could handle. We learned early that we could get away with a few things but knew not to press our luck too far. You know how girls are anyway. Tattletales! Yep, girls are quick to go tell, but my sisters were cool, I reckon.

Like most of the little kids in our town, we didn't have any fancy toys or bikes or anything of the sort, so we used our imaginations and were creative with whatever we could find around the farm. Some days we would just play games with one another. There were times when we would find some rope, old wood, or milk crates and really do something fun. It's amazing how imaginative you can be when you don't have lavish toys like the kids who had money. And living on the farm, we could get into a lot of mischief. If nothing else came to mind when we were bored, I'd just yell, "Let's chase chickens and see who can beat 'em!"

We didn't have much, and most of what we had was used up quickly. By the end of the month, food was scarce, but we were happy and content with our simple lifestyle. All was pretty good—until Pa's accident.

Unexpected Danger Ahead

As I recall from a geology lesson I had in school and from what Pa used to tell us, the mines were made of anthracite coal, where seams are locked in the folded layers of rock that make up the geology of Northeastern Pennsylvania. This formation made it dangerous and difficult to mine. The tunnels and shafts driven into the ground were often at steep angles that forced miners to crawl up or down the mine tunnels to get to the coal. Certain parts of the mine were worked with safety lamps. Explosions often occurred, injuring the miners in any number of ways from minor to serious to even death. Oftentimes, the blast would cause the supporting timbers and rocks to fall on the workers, overtaking even the strongest of men.

One cold, blistery winter day, a big news report broke saying that a premature ignition while setting an explosive blasting cap to dislodge embedded coal had blown the mine shaft, trapping and killing several of the miners. I remember that very well because Pa was one of the workers. It took days to get help to him and the others. By the time the rubble was removed, more support beams added, and the way cleared, a few of the men had already died. Even more were barely clinging to their hope of survival. Fortunately for our family, Pa was one of the survivors, but the weight of the fallen support timbers had crushed his spine, leaving him paralyzed from the waist down and wheelchair bound. Of course, he had no insurance.

That was the start of the deterioration of our loving family because now Ma had to do a lot of odd jobs for other folks while still maintaining the household. Bills really piled up from the accident and put us into heavy debt. Consider one day you're the breadwinner for your family, and then life happens, and you can't even afford to buy more than a half loaf of bread, a quarter stick of butter, one egg, and a cup of milk.

Pa was never the same after the accident. I guess none of us were. Since Pa started spending most of his time drinking more than anything else, I went searching for a way to bring in some money to help with the bills and put some food on the table while not causing problems with my schoolin'. My two other brothers did most of the farm chores in the evening while my sisters helped Ma wash clothes and do some sewing for other folks.

I was only twelve when I started working at Jackson's Corner Store. Old Man Jackson was a grumpy fellow who, most of the time, didn't seem to remember that I was only twelve. I did everything from mopping the floors to bagging to stocking the shelves and making a few deliveries. But he paid me, and we needed every little bit of money for the family.

I recall the first time I walked into the store and asked Old Man Jackson if he needed any help. He looked down at me with his long, straggly, white beard; peered through his spectacles with a frightful look; and said, "Boy, you look a might bit scrawny. Do you think yer strong enough to handle working here?" I told him I was plenty strong enough for any job he had for me.

He worked me very hard, and after a while he got used to having me around the store. On Fridays, after we closed the store and I finished mopping up, he'd give me a box filled with food and other items and say, "Boy, take this here stuff home to yer Ma."

I would just nod and say, "Yes, sir." Old Man Jackson always seemed to put enough food in the box to hold us until the next Friday.

I worked there with Old Man Jackson until I graduated from high school, so I never had to work a day in the mines like some of the other boys my age. Working in the mines had messed up my Pa, and I didn't want the same to happen to me. I had other plans for my life, though I wasn't sure what they were yet!

It was hard work to help support the family and go to school, but Ma reminded us that we needed our brains full so we could make something out of ourselves. So, I studied hard and did my best because I knew I didn't want to work in Jackson's store or at the mines for the rest of my life. I wanted to do something that would make my Ma and Pa really proud of me. I wanted to be able to buy them one of those fancy houses, one where we didn't have to farm the land for somebody else. After finishing high school, I couldn't wait to find the fastest thing moving out of town. I didn't care where it took me, as long as it was anywhere outside of Pennsylvania. Anywhere away from the memories. Anywhere that would allow me to be my own man!

Hit the Dirt, Lady

Since money was still tight, Uncle Sam had the best answer for helping fulfill my desires—I joined the army. I raised my hand, took the oath, and off I went out of the hills and familiar surroundings here in Pennsylvania straight to Fort Benning, Georgia. I thought the southern lifestyle and change of scenery would offer me exactly the escape I needed.

Once I got there, it seemed as if everyone liked to pick on the mountain man, as if saying, "Let's see what Rick Bosley is made of." I remember the first day of basic training. I jumped off the bus along with the other sixty or so misguided fellas much like myself. I guess I can laugh about it now, but we all must have had a similar bewildered look on our faces. Fort Benning was nothing like being back at home. Before I got there, folks told me how beautiful Georgia was. Well, during basic training, we didn't get to take sightseeing tours. The only sights we saw were the barracks, woods, and swampy areas on the base. Yes, you guessed it: Fort Benning really was not a place to collect neat postcards. My eyes captured everything around me, and it all seemed new, inspiring, and quite different, but not in an exciting way like when you are on vacation somewhere and discover new picturesque sights. *No!* This was more like, *what am I getting myself into?* Well, reality didn't take long to awaken me from my dreamy state!

The drill sergeant looked at me and commenced a verbal assault upon my poor eardrums as if he thought that I needed this abuse. Maybe it was my long, wiry hair and colorful T-shirt and tattered blue jeans, but whatever aroused his attention toward me, it started almost immediately. With the skill and accuracy of a prize fighter, he hit me with a barrage of insults. He was shouting so loud at me that I really couldn't make out all the words except "*Hit the dirt, lady!*" I could tell he really enjoyed my pain and suffering. In fact, I believe I was making his day. From that day on, for his entertainment, I would frequently engage in more push-ups and more time with my face in the dirt than any of my fellow troopers.

I was almost tempted to have my time recorded for *The Guinness Book of World Records.* Could you imagine? "Breaking news! This is Walter Cronkite, and today, we have a young army recruit from the coal, and today, we have a young army recruit from the coal mines of Pennsylvania who has just set the Guinness Record for the most push-ups accomplished in a twenty-four-hour period in a dirt pit!" I'd go back home famous. "Hey, boy! Aren't you that record holder or something like that? How's bout you show us?"

Well, on second thought, maybe that's not exactly what I want to be famous for! I trained to be an infantryman or ground pounder. I guess I was thrilled about the possibility of really doing something important in my life. I was actually pretty good at it. I reckon some of that shooting squirrel with Pa had helped me to develop a good eye. "A dead eye," some would say. Pa would say, "Boy, if you can shoot a ground squirrel without blowing it to pieces, then you can hit anything."

I recall one day, while we were in the final phase of training, the senior drill instructor for our platoon came up to me while I was cleaning my weapon. I was surprised and a little thrilled when he asked me if I wanted to blow up things—simply put, an army career in demolition. When I said, "You betcha," the drill instructor told me that he would check on it for me. A few days before graduation, they posted a listing of names and duty stations. Next to my name was Fort Bragg, North Carolina. I guess the drill instructor had worked things out for me because I was being assigned to an explosive ordnance disposal (EOD) platoon.

Living on the Edge

Talk about a bunch of highly motivated, skilled soldiers who were dedicated to being the very best at blowing up stuff. I hit it off really good with Corporal Denny O'Reilly, this short, stout soldier from somewhere in Tennessee who talked morning, noon, and night about bombs. Denny had this country twang to his voice like any minute he was going to start singing "Good Ol' Boy," you know, the theme song from the *Dukes of Hazzard*.

Denny had been in the army about four years now, so he knew a lot more than I did about the rules and regulations. Denny and I bunked together, which made it easy to learn all about demolition. He liked talking; he was one of those fellas with the gift of gab. Denny grew up with sisters, so I guess he treated me like the little brother he never had. We could talk about anything. One minute, he'd say, "Rick, square away your uniform" or "Tighten up your bunk." Then he'd start talking about leadership and blowing up things, and before I knew it, he was talking about his favorite movie and how he wished he had a shot of moonshine and some chaw.

One day I asked him, "Denny, what is chaw?"

Denny said in the country twang of his, "Boy, don't you know nothing? Look here and learn! This stuff in this tin can is what we call chewing tobacco! It's okay for just a pinch between your cheek and gum, but chaw is almost like a hard stick of tobacco, and you chew a big heap of it. It really gets you juiced up in the mouth, you know what I mean?"

In fact, one day while we were just sitting around, Denny gave me some of his chewing tobacco to try and *yuck*. I was spitting tobacco grind from my mouth for a couple of days. I guess it's not for everybody, especially not for me. Denny, he chewed and spit all day long. He said it relaxed him while he was working.

After four years in EOD, I believe Denny knew as much as the sarge about explosives. He always said, "Rick, you must be as alert as a cat on the prowl, seeing and listening for everything, because when you stop doing that—*boom!*"

Denny taught me everything I needed to know about bombs. He told me about Claymore mines, cluster bombs, C-4, and Bouncing Betties. I think Denny enjoyed keeping me on edge. For anything that could explode and blow-up things, Denny was definitely the expert.

In 1968, I received orders to go to Vietnam with one of the Infantry Divisions. Now going on my third year in the army, it was painful leaving such a good friend like Denny. But duty called, and off we both went on our separate ways. I heard later that he was so good at blowing up stuff and the enemy that the army made him an instructor and sent him to EOD school to train officers.

I, along with the other soldiers headed to Vietnam with me, had to fly to sunny California to catch a ship out of Alameda, near Oakland. Now this was living. Yep, a long way from the coal mines now. California! Land of Hollywood, big stars, and absolutely no coal mines. This was getting really exciting because now my career in the army was taking me places, I'd only dreamed about and heard about. I knew my pa would sure be proud of his son.

Me and a few of the guys, we hit the town hard knowing that we had a midnight curfew and would then leave in the morning. Well, things like this normally occur only once in a lifetime, and it was my time. We set out to catch some sights, dry out the town, and kiss as many pretty girls as we could. Everybody loves a man in uniform. We must have hit every club, bar, and joint that had bright neon lights telling us to come on in and make pure fools of ourselves. And you know what; I believe we did just that.

At one time during the night before everything got all fuzzy, I met this beautiful, blonde lady named Ginger. Talk about a woman who looked like she'd just walked right off the pages of one of them magazines filled with all those pretty models. This was love at first sight, or so I thought, never having been in love before! We danced, laughed, and drank up all my money, and then she left me and moved to another soldier sitting at the bar. I got mad and was about to go punch his lights out when one of the guys dared me to drink this bottle of stuff that had a worm in the bottom of the bottle. Forget the woman; this was a challenge, and I was the right soldier to tackle it. I think I did it... hard to say since I don't remember much of anything that happened after that. Matter of fact, I really don't know how we made it back to report in by midnight for our Cinderella curfew. I guess the cabbies knew exactly where to dump us drunks—out of town and minus the remaining bucks in our wallets that we hadn't spent already.

The next morning, somehow, we all boarded the ship, stumbling up the gangplank, each of us hungover and still reeking of last night's fun times. And as the ship slowly drifted away from the pier into the bay, it brought back memories of how packed we were also on that bus ride to basic training at Fort Benning. Many of the guys sat on their racks in the belly of the ship praying for safety, for God's protection, and for their seasickness to quit soon so they could eat something. More than anything they prayed just to live and return back to their families. I looked around at all these American heroes who seemed to have forgotten what they were trained to do. They seemed to have forgotten what their training really meant. It meant that we were the best fighting machines ever and that the enemy would dread the day that they messed with us Americans. I didn't need God. Only the weak soldiers did all that praying stuff.

Pa used to tell me, "All that church stuff don't do no good except for women, children, and old folks."

I'd stick out my chest and say, "Pa, I'm a man like you, so we stick together!"

Pa would smile in acknowledgment that I'd learned my lesson well. I didn't need God. I had my rifle by my side, and that was all I needed to stay between me, the enemy, and death. And if I needed something a little more, I was EOD and could blow up any threat.

I could imagine people saying, "Watch out! Rick Bosley is coming to town, and he's packing some heavy-duty stuff and ain't afraid to use it!"

11

It seemed to take forever for us to get to land again, but as we approached the beachfront, I found myself looking, almost staring, at all the faces around me on that ship. Each one seemed to be silently wishing that he was somewhere else but here. A gloom blanketed the whole area, and the eerie veil of death loomed all around. In the distance, I heard the sounds of war, and for a moment, a gut feeling came over me that this was not going to be a picnic or walk in the park. I thought, *I better make sure I pack extra heavy for this!*

Not a Walk in the Park

My unit moved north to Chu Lai and joined up with two other divisions to add our contributions to this war. Our EOD platoon was rather small at thirty strong, and we divided up to go out with whoever was the lead unit for that day and needed us. Well, let me tell you, training is one thing, but being in the bush really shows what kind of man you are: schoolboy or seasoned soldier. By this point, I was feeling mighty salty.

One day I headed out with a patrol, and there was one of them righteous fellas, you know, one of them Bible-thumpers. You know the type, always spouting about fire and brimstone, love and peace, and a bunch of other stuff like that. Well, he had this look on his face, I guess of assurance in something, and he had the audacity to come up to me and say, "I'll pray for you, Rick." Then to pile more on, he added, "Jesus will protect us." He sounded like my mama.

Before he could say another crazy word to me, I looked him straight in his eyes and said, "I have all I need right here—my rifle, my bayonet, and some grenades. Save your prayers for somebody that really needs them."

Well, it didn't take long for us to be in the thick of battle. Just like the song, bombs were bursting in the air, with the rockets' red glare and white flashes all around us. Now this was what separated the men from the boys. I thought, *Yep, look at me: I'm fully equipped with my combat gear—steel pot, rifle, flak jacket, hand grenades, and enough bullets to do some real damage to the enemy. Just like a turkey shoot back home.* As I sat there in a foxhole, all that came to mind was those games at carnivals, the kind where they hand you a pop rifle with those ducks and things moving and spinning all around and the carnival guy says, "All you have to do is hit all the targets to win a prize."

I was beginning to get that feeling. I had the rifle in my hand, it was loaded, and I was ready! Ready and waiting for one of them Vietcong (VC) or Charlie, as we have nicknamed the enemy, to raise his head and let me shoot it off like a gopher. I would just sit here in my covered fighting hole, take steady aim, and get ready to pluck off any VC in my area of this hot jungle. In the distance, I heard the cries of other men who were under fire. All of a sudden, an endless stream of artillery fire and explosions erupted all around me, breaking the silence that once blanketed this jungle. It got so heavy that the lieutenant motioned for us to move out and reposition ourselves in order to help out the others and gain back the advantage from Charlie.

War can be brutal on the mind and body. It's on-the-job training on a larger and more costly scale. You go to school and train to do it the textbook way, and maybe, if you're smart and listen real closely to someone who has been there and done it, you will have an advantage over the other guy. I had Denny and a few guys from my EOD platoon who had been here in the thick of things, and they told me about it. But until you were here, all that stuff was just a bunch of stories and fairy tales. I mean, this was for real now! As much as I would have liked to think that I was prepared and ready for anything, I saw the reality, and it wasn't pretty. Truly, death was all around me, and the bad part about this whole scene was that I wasn't dreaming. It was so smoky there in the jungle that I could hardly make out the good guys from the bad guys. My adrenaline was pumping, faster and faster, at a new all-time pace. "Hey, can you smell that?" one of my fellow soldiers asked. Nobody had warned me about the smell of death!

It seemed like only minutes had passed, but all over lay the bodies of fallen soldiers. It was hard to keep on moving and step over one of our own. I may have sat next to him on the boat ride over or in camp. He may have been that guy who wanted to pray for me and maybe had forgotten to pray for himself. Well, they'd send somebody else to collect our guys. I had to keep moving. I had something special for them VC! Shoot up and blow up Americans? No way! I had something for them, for sure!

As shock and fear overtook me, I forgot one crucial training tip that our platoon commander and Denny had stressed to us all: "Watch your step at all times!"

I heard a loud, audible click that was unmistakable to a trained EOD specialist as myself. Oops, too late. Sweat beads popped from my forehead. As the sound registered in my brain-housing group (as we say in the army for mind), my eyes flicked down to my feet. While overtaken by the events and my surroundings, I'd lost focus and had stepped right on top of one of Charlie's booby traps.

Minutes now seemed to transverse time and switched into slow-motion mode. In my mind, I said, *Okay, Rick, what are you going to do now?* I could hear the platoon coming but could not seem to utter a word. Some would say that fear had set in. Time seemed to take a pause; everything around me became silent except for the racing beat of my heart drumming through my chest. Now, all of a sudden, sweat started pouring out of me as though I had sprung a leak. As my life reeled before my eyes like a bad drive-in movie or Quentin Tarantino scene, the blasting sound rang out, and an incredible bright, white light and intense heat covered me as my body was hurled through the air, landing several yards away in one heaping pile.

It was such a shock, as you can imagine, almost like taking a plunge into a pool filled with ice water or, worse yet, ice-skating on a lake that seemingly is frozen over until you land on a spot that gives way underneath you. My mind suddenly shifted into panic mode.

Dead Man's Curve

While I lay there on the ground, memories again started to play loud and clear in my mind…I could see the time when Sammy Baker and I were riding our bikes and decided to take a dare and try some pretty acrobatic stuff, flying down Dead Man's Curve and jumping the ravine. People said that it could never be done because the hill coming down was nearly two thousand feet and then to propel across the ravine was thirty yards with a dangerous drop of more than five hundred feet. With the wind to our backs, it was like we were flying through the air—at least, I was. Sammy chickened out, hit the brakes, and decided not to jump, but I made it. Of course, I busted up my bike, flipped over the handlebars, and broke my arm and busted up my nose. But I did it.

Just like then, the pain didn't hit me all at once as I lay there in the jungle, unable to move. As I continued to wait for someone to come help me, an awful stream of pain alerted my brain-housing group that I was hurt bad. The only problem was that unlike with the bike jump, this time I wasn't able to get up and move. My mind was telling me to get up, shake it off, and keep on moving like a good soldier, but it was like a weight on me kept me pressed to the ground. I could hear someone call, "*Medic!*" but I wasn't sure if it was for me or not. I could see and hear and feel, so I thought I must be okay. The doc and my sarge rushed over to check on me—I guess to help me off the ground. Sarge kept asking me to tell him my name and platoon number. I thought maybe he was injured too because he already knew me, but I went along with the game. I guess it was to keep my mind off of the doc sticking me with the morphine and putting tourniquets on my legs. Suddenly, a helicopter landed near me, and all I could see was dust flying everywhere. It was very painful being jerked up and down as they ran with me to the helicopter and then put me inside. Then, lights out!

When I awoke, I recall wondering if I had died and gone to heaven. I'd never thought about it before, but it sure looked really nice and bright and clean with white everywhere. Then I saw two nurses next to me taking my vitals, so I started to feel pretty good about myself. This was great! One moment I was running around the hot, sweaty jungle with my army buds on one side and the Vietcong on the other, and now I was in the midst of angels. Somebody would think I'd gotten religion in the jungle. It must have been the drugs, I guess. I felt good, but why were all these people around me? I was getting a lot of attention. I was being swarmed by several doctors and nurses, and one of the doctors said, "Well, let's get this soldier into the operating room and see if we can save him!" A whole lot was going on all around me, but I didn't care. I was feeling really good about now. The angels had given me the *good stuff!*

The field corpsmen had evidently bundled me together into the bag hoping maybe something there would be salvageable. I guess I was a sight! One leg was barely attached, and the other was completely gone. I found out later that they'd searched for the other one but had never found it.

Days later I awoke in my hospital bed. The first thing I noticed was that there was something definitely different about me. It took me a few more days and no anesthesia and very little drugs in my system to come to the realization that both of my legs were gone. My leg that had been barely attached had been amputated. I guess I wouldn't make that mistake of being careless and stepping on an enemy mine again. I guess Denny was right! I guess the next time I'll know better.

"What do I do now?"

Reflective Key Verse

> Hear my cry, O God; listen to my prayer. From the ends
> of the earth, I call to you, I call as my heart grows faint;
> lead me to the rock that is higher than I. For you have
> been my refuge, a strong tower against the foe. I long to
> dwell in your tent forever and take refuge in the shelter
> of your wings.
>
> —Psalm 61:1–4, NIV

Spiritual Moment

Let's call on a biblical character to help make this story real to you. One such person that immediately comes to mind is King Jehoshaphat, fourth king of the kingdom of Judah. Here was a man who had begun to lead the people back to worshiping the true and living God. Suddenly a warning comes to ears of King Jehoshaphat concerning the gathering of his enemies, the Moabites, to attack him. The Bible says he was afraid. What is important is what he did with his fear, concern, and anxiety. Immediately he gathered the people together and prayed, "O our

God, will You not judge them? For we have no power against this great multitude that is coming against us; nor do we know what to do, but our eyes *are* upon You." (2 Chronicles 20:12). A prophet gave Jehoshaphat the Lord's answer: "You will not have to fight this battle. Take up your positions; stand firm and see the deliverance the Lord will give you, Judah and Jerusalem. Do not be afraid; do not be discouraged. Go out to face them tomorrow, and the Lord will be with you!" (2 Chronicles 20:17, NIV)

Here is a picture of a vulnerable people who don't know what to do, who are completely dependent upon God. Now let's take a moment and place ourselves in a similar situation; think of an issue or problem you may be going through or dealing with right now. You are at a time of need, and here is what you need to know: God answered the prayer of the king and dramatically altered his circumstances by destroying his enemies. Remember, you can turn to God in prayer in desperate circumstances; God will hear your cry and miraculously change your condition.

Life Challenge

So many of our honored veterans like Rick experienced extreme hardship and emotional disorientation during their valiant service only to be thrown back into a society that cares little about how much of their lives they sacrificed for their country.

Have you ever been in what appeared to be an impossible situation? Have you ever desperately needed something, but it seemed you would never, have it? Have you ever thought there was no future for you? Well, if you've ever felt that way, then you need to know that God can answer prayer and can turn situations around. He can turn people around and, when necessary, can even change the course of nature. It has been said, "If you are swept off your feet, it's time to get on your knees."

CHAPTER 2

Johnny's Story: Just Trying to Get Mine Now

And let the peace of God rule in your hearts,

to which also you were called in one body; and be thankful.

—Colossians 3:15

Hard Streets of South Central

That do you do when your sense of freedom, wild running, and being your own man is suddenly halted, like the impact of a car racing at top speed and suddenly, out of control, slamming into a wall? What do you do when you get caught up in life and life has you spinning like a top, just spiraling around like a whirlwind until you run out of momentum and topple over? I hadn't imagined that I, Johnny "Black Jack" Taylor, of all people, would now be facing a lifetime behind bars. But the sirens blast louder and louder as they close in on me. A few moments go by, and from a megaphone someone bellows, "This is the police: you're under arrest. Come out with your hands up!"

What should I do? This will be the third strike against me if I turn myself in. Yes, I've been arrested quite a few times but only gone to jail twice. I can see it now. The judge will just throw the book at me and lock me away for good. No attorney will even bother because I've been labeled a *career criminal.*

The irony of the moment is that I've escaped death several times during my somewhat-short twenty-two years of life, a life molded by my close association with the streets in which I ran. Yes, you may say that I am a product of my environment, growing up on the hard, sometimes-treacherous ghetto streets of South-Central Los Angeles.

I grew up in the Compton area. It's hard to imagine any areas in California having ghettos and driving through Compton during the day with the tall, beautiful palm trees and sunshine that seems like it never ends, you would wonder what people were talking about. But it becomes a different place when the sun goes down. Here in South Central, "the Jungle," many learn to respect the harsh streets. It is not unusual to be in your home minding your own business and hear gunfire ringing just outside the window. You might even say that I am a product of a society built on rhetoric and ridicule. Who says that a young black man must grow up bad? Who says that a young black man from the ghetto is destined for prison life? Who says that a young black man will never amount to anything? The world, that's who, but who says the world is right?

The first time I was arrested, I was fourteen years old. It was 1995. Chico, Mario, and Jose, some Hispanic bullies from around the way, had been picking on a few of the kids in the hood at school and around the playground, so my friends and I decided to teach them a lesson in respect. So, I grabbed my toy BB gun—you know, one of those models that look like the real thing, a real .45—and joined together with a couple of my boys, and we went down to Crenshaw Boulevard. It didn't take long before we ran into those same guys, and I pulled out the gun to scare them. Man, they were shaking like leaves. One of them wet his pants. All the while, we were yelling at them and letting them know that the next time we heard of them messing with anybody on our turf, we'd settle the score in another way. That's when the cops drove by, saw it, jumped out of their cars, pulled their guns, and made all of us drop to the ground. They let the others go but handcuffed me, threw me in the back of the police car, and turned me over to the county juvenile detention center. I was released a couple of hours later after they sorted out the paperwork and discovered it was only a BB gun. They then turned me over to my mom. Unfortunately for me, this was not a wake-up call or my last time at juvie or in any other prison setting! As it seems to be the case with most boys in my hood, this was my step from childhood into manhood, and I was about to take a giant leap.

Well, news in the Jungle passes quickly, and before you knew it, I was approached by one of the gang lieutenants in our hood. His name is not important now, but you can believe I was a little scared at first. He quickly told me that he'd heard how I was protecting our turf and that he wanted me to be legit. Let me tell you, when they come to you and tell you that you should be with them, you don't say no. It seemed that gang- banging was about to be the life for me.

The second time I was arrested, wouldn't you know it, was only about four months later. It came as part of my gang initiation. Some of the gang members got me high—I guess it was for courage—knocked me around a bit, and then told me to go make a hit. So, me and my boys found an opening in a gate behind one of the local audio-stereo stores and crawled inside to steal a few things and show we had the stuff. Instead of coming out the same way we'd come in, we decided to just walk out the back door since our arms were full of car stereos and speakers. And coming down the alley was a police cruiser. Caught again, a bunch of stupid kids!

A year later I had moved up to hot-wiring and jacking cars. My mom thought it would be best that I spend some time with my pops up in New York. I didn't really care about being with him since I hadn't seen him since I was little, but she thought it would be the best way of keeping me out of prison or from getting gunned down in the streets before I reached my seventeenth birthday.

Out of the Hood

Although I really didn't want to leave my homeys and everything, I was familiar with in South Central, it was almost exciting thinking about the opportunities ahead of me in the big city of New York. I can recall leaving the California area only a couple of times. Once we all took a family road trip to Arizona to see a ball game. And another time when I was younger, Mom put me and my brother on a bus to visit our grandparents in Alabama. Even in the country, a kid can get in trouble if he wants to, and I was no exception. Country life tends to be slow and, to me, boring, so you have to create your own spice. You can say me and my brother got into our share of trouble.

Pops lived in East Brooklyn near Queens in a nice little house unlike the cramped apartment I grew up in. Brooklyn reminded me of South Central in a few ways, mainly by the fact that it was a big city with a lot of people of different ethnic groups and cultures. What I didn't know was that Pops and Mom had already made up their minds that I would stay with Pops until I graduated from high school, whether I liked it or not.

The first thing Pops did when I arrived was read me the riot act. He sat me down and told me where and where not to go, what time he wanted me in the house every day, and what he expected from me. He also warned me about the crime in this area. Unlike South Central, you couldn't necessarily tell the good guys from the bad guys by their dress code or colors. In fact, even if they were black, white, Hispanic, Asian, or whatever, it did not mean too much. Crime in New York took on the persona of many races, cultures, social settings, and economic status. But don't let me leave you thinking that there were no distinctions here in New York. Believe me, if you ran up on a group of young people and they were dressed identically, it probably wasn't a sporting group!

Life in the Big Apple

My earlier run-in with the law, gang lifestyle, and bad-boy attitude completely changed once I had settled in Brooklyn. I started making new friends, tried out and made the varsity football team, and even was doing pretty good with my grades. High school was great! And believe me: if I got out of line the slightest, Pops was all over me. I thought living in the streets of South Central made me tough, but Pops was tougher. I learned quickly that his way was the only way in his house, and you better believe I followed willingly! Pops worked long hours driving one of those trash trucks for the city sanitation department. It wasn't the most lavish job and definitely wasn't the kind of job where he had to wear a suit and tie. Pops had to be on the job at 5:00 a.m. and normally didn't get home till after 7:00 p.m. Pops worked hard and took good care of those things that belonged to him. He had a '72 Chevy Nova that didn't look like much, but it moved, so Pops was satisfied. The neighbors were all nice and looked out for one another. Unlike Compton, life was quiet and beautiful here. It just had an atmosphere that was so different for me and kept me in the right frame of mind to do the right thing!

Life was great! My closest friends—Kenny and Eric—and I played football together. We were also in a lot of the same classes together. Pops liked them and had met their parents, so he did not mind me spending time at their homes after school. They all had pretty nice homes with both parents while it was just me and Pops. In fact, folks around the neighborhood began calling Kenny, Eric, and me the Three Amigos because everywhere we went, we were all three together. At school—together, after-school activities—together, store—together; we were just that close.

Our senior year at high school things changed slightly because we all starting seeing girls and hanging out with them, but most of the time, we even did that together. My girl, Linda, had just moved into the neighborhood about three months ago, and we hit it off from the first time we met. It all happened at school. She had just arrived here, and she found herself having trouble locating her algebra class. It so happened that I was in that same class, so I showed her how to get to the class. Actually, it worked out perfectly because algebra was not my best subject. In fact, I was failing, and that would affect my grade average and potential for a scholarship, and I would be dropped from the football team. Pops would not be happy! On the other hand, Linda was a mathematical genius, so she tutored me. I started doing a lot of things with her, and her mom let me come over to eat dinner with them since Pops worked late some nights and I was definitely not by any stretch a chef. I was a champ with a microwave, frozen meals, and hot dogs; anything more than that and I had a mess on my hands.

It's amazing how life can easily change. Less than two years ago, I had been in South Central living the thug life, running with gangs, committing crimes, and trying to stay alive on the streets. Now I was a high school senior with pretty good grades and was playing sports.

Pops told me, "You keep it up and you'll get a scholarship to go to college." He made sure I took every test and seized every opportunity to be competitive, and I did it! I played football, baseball, and basketball and even joined the chess team for a semester. Pops had taught me how to play, and I figured joining the team would help sharpen my game. Those guys were skilled and had played for years; I was definitely not in their league. Football was my sport. I guess all the running we did in South Central from the cops and other thugs that didn't like us had paid off and made me rather fast. So I played cornerback on defense because I was fast but liked hitting rather than getting hit. Our team was very good too. The best thing was that now I had a lot of friends because of football, but none like my boys Eric and Kenny. Yes, we were definitely the Three Amigos!

The Price of Smokes

Pops yelled up the stairs, "Johnny, before you go to practice, run to the store, and pick me up some smokes."

"Not a problem," I said. "I'll go grab the fellas, and we'll be right back."

I was only able to find Kenny; Eric had already left for football practice. So Kenny and I walked down the block to the 7-Eleven since it was close by. The store clerk, Bobby, a schoolmate of ours, was sweeping the store parking lot. We talked for a bit, you know, school and sports stuff, and then went inside to get Pops's smokes.

We didn't notice the car, an old model Impala pull up in the parking lot the same time we were going into the store. Two guys stepped out of the car and entered the 7-Eleven behind us. Bobby put his broom and dustpan against the side of the building and followed the two guys into the store. As Bobby walked behind the counter area, one of the men pulled a sawed-off shotgun from under his coat, pointed it at Bobby, and ordered him to empty the register into a paper bag. The other guy pulled out a gun and told me and Kenny to get down on the floor, shut up, and not move. All I could do was lie down with my face against the floor, scared and hoping somebody walked by outside and noticed something in here and called the cops.

The robbers were shouting, and Bobby was crying and trying to get the register open. Then all of a sudden, Kenny jumped up and tried to grab the robber nearest the door. I looked up, and everything seemed to immediately switch into slow motion or a scene from *The Matrix*. A shot rang out and propelled Kenny into one of the shelves. The other guy with the shotgun snatched the bag of money from the cashier and then turned and told his partner, "Let's get out of here and not smoke nobody else."

They burst out the store, jumped into their car, and drove off, speeding down the road. I was so stunned by the chain of events that I stayed on the floor until the cops got there; just looking at my friend's lifeless body slumped over some cans and bread. The cops and medics showed up about the same time. An ambulance took Kenny to the hospital while the police talked to both me and Bobby and asked us for descriptions of the robbers and the car and anything else we could remember. All that I could think about was my friend being shot and wondering if he was going to be all right. His parents and my pops were called, and everybody hurried to the hospital to make sure he was going to be all right. I remember sitting there in that hospital emergency room waiting area wondering if Kenny was okay. His parents were crying, and

Pops was pacing the floor. Eric and Linda tried to console me, but it was like I was in another time zone or something. I really couldn't hear or understand what they were saying to me. Besides, Eric hadn't been there when we all should have been together. If he had been, maybe Kenny would be okay.

Kenny's mom all of a sudden said, "We should hold hands and pray now."

I looked up at her and said a little too loudly, "Pray? What will that do? God didn't jump in and stop the bullet before it hit Kenny, and you want me to pray?"

I jumped up and stormed out of the waiting room. Everyone seemed rather shocked by my statement, and silence filled the room once again. Moments later, I saw the doctor step out and tell Kenny's parents something. I hurried back into the waiting room, and the faces and tears were all I needed to realize what they had been told… Kenny had died! The funeral was sad, as expected. It was a gloomy, overcast day. Everyone was either crying or just plain overwhelmed by the fact that Kenny had died. Kenny had been one of the better kids. He'd grown up in a fine home, had never been in trouble, and had been getting ready to graduate high school with so much ahead of him. He had received an academic scholarship to attend Cornell University. Now it was over. In one shattering moment, his life had ended. And worse yet, the cops still hadn't found the gunmen. No clues. No leads. No nothing. What good was the law? In fact, I knew how I could find those guys and get some payback for my boy Kenny. Pops may not like it, but I had to do what I had to do, because it could have been me! Maybe it should have been me there in that pretty casket, me lying there instead of Kenny. Maybe, but it wasn't.

Black Jack Is Back

Since Eric and my other school friends were nothing like me, I needed to connect with some dudes who lived like I used to live and thought like I used to think. I needed guys who knew the street game and could hook me up with the right connections. I knew I had only a couple more months and I'd be graduating. I also knew that Pops would not approve of me seeking vengeance and connecting with the type of people who would do it and not blink an eye. I knew that I'd worked hard to get scholarships to a few good colleges and play ball, but none of that could change the fact that my friend Kenny was no longer here. Maybe it really should have been me since I was the messed-up kid from the hood who should have been dead or in jail a long time ago anyway. What a change! With my mind on getting back into the thug life, it seemed that I now saw people that I could identify with all over. A few days after the funeral, I decided to not conceal my gang tattoos and walked down the street with no shirt. This way some other gangster could identify me and bring me into his family. Or I might just be ignored because folk around here didn't know or understand. Or I could be mistaken for a soldier boogying through their turf trying to take over, and I could get jumped or shot myself. I'd find out one way or another. Well, luck was on my side. I ran into a few guys down at a bar, and we talked about the shooting at the 7-Eleven, how it was my friend who'd been shot and how the cops hadn't done anything about it. This guy walked over to me—I'll call him T-Bone for now—looked me over, noticed my tattoos, and asked me where I was from. I told him Compton. He said that he used to run in Watts with his cousin and that after prison in San Quentin, he'd decided to move and stay here in Brooklyn. T-Bone recruited me there on the spot into his gang. It didn't take me long at all to be reintroduced into the life of gangbanging, only this was New York style! I decided to drop out of school, quit the football team, and burst the dream bubble on my college plans. I even stopped seeing Linda and started running with T-Bone and his boys. It was like a family reunion, and I was finally reuniting with some distant relatives.

As I learned, T-Bone had a heavy rep and controlled most of the East Side turf with a large network of soldiers. He was mainly a criminal businessman with a thirst for power, but he was savvy enough not to be targeted by other crime families or the law. T-Bone had built an empire and transformed a few city blocks into a well-defended center of operations for controlling and manipulating the growing crime wave he headed. In fact, T-Bone once said his ambition was to "rule the Bronx and Harlem one day." You might say that he was respected and admired as a gangster legend.

I'd made it! It was high times for me now. No more small-time, penny-ante crime. This was nothing like what I did in South Central. T-Bone explained everything to me, what I needed to do and his expectations for me, and said, "Kid, welcome to the big league." No more hot-wiring cars, breaking into stores to steal, shoplifting, or mugging people. This was organized crime. This was what made the headlines of newspapers and the top stories on the evening news. I began to feel like I now could be what I was cut out to be, for real. Black Jack was back and twice the threat I had been.

Before I knew it, I hit the streets, took up residence in the spot T-Bone wanted me to control, and began my new life. Everything that my life had become while living in Brooklyn was now a thing of the past... no need for graduation, no need for school, no need for scholarships, no need for friends, and no more need for Pops. I had a new family now, and family took care of each other. And I needed family to help me dish out a little payback for the death of my friend.

For the first time in my short life, I was introduced to the drug world. Yes, I know they had some drugs and crack dealers back in South Central. They had some numbers rackets and prostitution too. But this was the heavy stuff—drugs, narcotics, serious gambling, and guns for hire. The big time, baby!

We owned the night, and nothing moved unless we allowed it. In fact, nighttime was our time! The city did not sleep at this hour; the streets belong to us. Drugs, liquor, women, and plenty of firepower—life was cheap. T-Bone always said, "Keep your head up, and watch your back. Don't let the next bullet have your name on it!"

Living Just Enough

The drug trade was nothing if not cynical, and now I was back in the game behind the scenes, making deals and dodging death, caught up in a web of deceit that I manipulated so skillfully. This time, possibly, there was no way out.

Almost a year went by, and as a loyal banger, I'd earned T-Bone's trust and confidence. T-Bone had me setting up the deals, meeting with the local Mexicans and Italians, pushing the tons of drugs for the insatiable appetites of addicts, and trafficking guns and loot. I had become a big-time player with no fear of death, simply living the life each and every day. It was a life filled with evil, but who cared, I was getting mine.

Speaking of getting mine, a few more months passed, and as Lady Luck would have it, me and a couple of my soldiers were hanging around the hood and happened to overhear these dudes talking about a heist they'd done at a 7-Eleven store a while back and how they'd had to show some young schoolboy that they meant business by blasting him. Well, my heart seemed to stop beating, as my ears turned up like radar, seeming to adjust themselves for a more attentive listening posture. These guys just kept running their mouths and bragging. In fact, they told the story so well it gave me flashbacks as though I was reliving the whole scene again. Then one of the guys said, "Yeah, and I wanted to pop the other chump on the floor, but I think he was crying for his mama!"

Can you imagine these guys talking with no care of the life they took, trying to make it look like they were so tough? Well, before they could do any begging, any pleading, or crying like babies, I said, "This is for my boy Kenny," and my boys and I took matters into our own hands, right there on the spot. No arrest. No trial. We were the judge and jury, and the verdict was simple. An eye for an eye was street creed.

Oh yes, Black Jack was back in the game, and now it was for keeps. Drugs, gambling, stealing, and now murder added to my résumé. Man! I felt like I was important again. I had new boys that now respected me for being like T-Bone, all action and no mercy. Definitely after this there was no going back to playing ball with my neighborhood friends or holding hands at the ice cream parlor with Linda. Yep! What was I thinking? College scholarships, a career, little house, wife and kids? Not this guy! I was Black Jack, and I had the whole world to gain and overtake now if I wanted it. Say what you will, but this was my time, and I was going to get mine. Laid-out pad, fancy ride or two, fine ladies all around me, jewelry, and all the green I ever could imagine.

I was on my way to the big time! What could stop me? In fact, I could be more than T-Bone. T-Bone wanted to rule the Bronx and Harlem, but I could be one of the big bosses of New York. You know, just like the Mafia, I could be the head of one of the largest black crime waves in all of New York and possibly into New Jersey. All I needed to do was build my reputation! In fact, here was the plan. First, I'd build up my rep, building my name alongside of T-Bone's so when people spoke his name, they knew me too. From there it would be easy to step up and be feared by both the other crime organizations and the cops. Yes! And as my gang grew and became bigger and badder, we'd just take more and more turf until we controlled it all. You know, T-Bone wasn't going to be around long, and I was still young with my whole life ahead of me. This was the life, and there was no stopping me now. Yes, Black Jack was back!

This Is It

But then I heard sirens, and that brings us to where I am now, cornered by the cops. Somebody must have snitched about the shooting, and the worst part about it all is that I can still smell the gunpowder all over my hands. I'm not sure if it is pure adrenaline—maybe a sense of invincibility or some fear of the inevitable, I don't know—but now the same thought keeps running through my mind: *What should I do?* This will be my third strike if I turn myself in, and if I'm convicted of just the murder charges, not to mention the other crimes on my rap sheet, I'm done. The judge will lock me away for good because now I have murder added to my already-large resume, and the weapon is still in my hand. I've seen the *Godfather*, *Scarface*, *Dillinger*, and *Goodfellas*, you know the movies. Maybe if I shoot it out I can get away and escape to Canada or Mexico. Yes, I could sip fancy drinks on the beach in Jamaica with my ladies. I could actually live pretty good. Or I could wind up dead on a cold slab in the morgue. *What should I do?*

Reflective Key Verse

And let the peace of God rule in your hearts, to which also you were called in one body; and be thankful.

—Colossians 3:15

Spiritual Moment

God speaks to us through His peace. Another way to translate the above verse is "Let God's peace act as an umpire in your lives, settling with finality all matters that arise."

God's peace can act as an umpire in your life. He can settle with finality what you should do. Here's how it works. Maybe you think that something is the will of God. Circumstantially, things have fallen into place. You begin to proceed, but then you have a complete lack of peace. Something inside of you is saying, "Don't do it."

A story in the Old Testament tells of a group of clever individuals known as Gibeonites who lived in Canaan. God had instructed Joshua not to make any deals with the inhabitants of the land, so the Gibeonites put on old shoes and clothes and pretended as though they had come from a distant country. They told Joshua they had come to enter into an agreement with him, and Joshua unknowingly struck a deal with his enemies because he failed to consult the Lord.

Things can look good outwardly, and everything can seem right. Be careful. Learn to listen to that still, small voice. Learn to pay attention to that peace, or lack of it, in your life because that is one of the ways God will lead you. When you're in the will of God, you will have His peace.

Life Challenge

Many times, in newspapers, on television, or anywhere with a discussion of statistics, people take a random or even purposeful look at people much like Johnny. Our society and media openly portray African American youths, especially males, as criminals, crime victims, and predators. Now add to that scenario the geographical area. Clearly, the perception regarding people of color lends itself to racial tension and reinforces stereotypes. Let's face it plainly. With limited job options, poor housing areas, welfare, the high cost of education, and economic recession, young African Americans often make bad choices because they view their condition as hopeless. The solution lies in the formidable representation of people of color through positive images throughout society. We need more people promoting high educational standards for our youth. We need more true father figures in homes. We need hardworking wage earners striving to be successful achievers, not expecting life to be given to them as a handout.

There are many temptations that can rob you of your livelihood and even your very soul if you allow them to. The world is filled with endless ghettos burdened with heartache, pain, sorrow, depression, hopelessness, and sadness. The key is being an overcomer and knowing what to sow, how to sow it, and where to sow.

It's hard when life makes suggestions that alter the direction of our lives, and we, without thought about the future consequences, jump right in and take the ride. Sometimes the ride ends up like a scene out of *The Fast and the Furious*—you know, trying to outrun everything only to find ourselves both disabled and unable to proceed until help comes our way or, worse yet, hopelessly swerving out of control and ending up in a sad state. The choice is ours to make. There's always a better option. We must learn to stop, think, and realize the future before it spells our end!

CHAPTER 3

Maria's Story: This Road Is Easier

Be sober, be vigilant; because your adversary the devil walks about like a roaring lion, seeking whom he may devour.

—1 Peter 5:8

No Place for a Lady

Life has a way of changing what you had in mind, rearranging your dreams, and landing you in the middle of "How did I get here?" When I was a child, people asked me, "What do you want to be when you grow up?" It's difficult to imagine what their reaction would have been if my answer had described what I have become. I wonder if my expectations were more than my capabilities. I only wanted to be better than the average Latina coming from my background and neighborhood. I'm at a loss for words. Let me set the record straight. Please walk with me as I share my story.

I push my shopping cart through this park here in Boyle Heights, the slums of Los Angeles; it holds everything I own, all my worldly goods. I don't have much, but I have no need for much right now. I'd leave this stuff in my home if I had one that was permanent and not just a cardboard box under a bridge overpass in a community with several similar structures. The clothes on my back and shoes on my feet are all I need for now. If I get cold, I have a coat that I found in a dumpster. It's amazing the nice things people will just throw out in the trash. One day I was just strolling down the street, and there it was in the trash… just for me. Dumpsters have become my shopping center. Everything I need and more… department store, shoe store, furniture store, and restaurant. I've become content just living my life. There's that look again!

Just a few short years ago, if you had walked up on me, I would have been either strung out on crack, drunk, or both. My husband had rejected me. I'd been sexually, physically, and emotionally abused. You don't live on skid row, do the things I've had to do to survive, and not experience the fear and violence that is bred on the streets. I was labeled "at risk" from the sheer reality that my condition kept me right here on the streets. In fact, not much mattered to me during that time in my life, but things are much better for me now. Yes, I'm still on the streets— homeless, jobless, penniless—but at least now, I have hope! I'm happy, and I'm comfortable. I'm in control now! There's that look again! Maybe you don't understand why I say that. Okay, if you have a few moments, have a seat with me on this bench, and let me tell you, my story.

Born in the USA

Stevie Wonder wrote a song that described Maria at birth: "Isn't she lovely… isn't she wonderful!" Just take a look at her, such a beautiful child! *She is our blessing! She's our precious pride and joy,* thought Anna,

Maria's mother. Right now, after giving birth Anna was thinking, *how can I raise this child by myself? It's been hard enough with the other two. We were just getting by, and now I have another one. How are we going to make it?* These questions and several others flow effortlessly from Anna's mind along with a parade of other despairing images of hopelessness and helplessness.

Well, the fact plainly was that my baby girl was now here, and the baby was so happy and pretty. Enough of the sad thoughts. It was time to introduce the newest addition to her brother, Marco, and sister, Merissa. "*No matter what happens or how tought it may get, I will hold this family together*," said Anna.

In the Beginning

My Mama and Papa were high school sweethearts. Wherever you went, you always saw Mario and Anna. Everyone knew that my Mama was Mario's girl, and my grandparents liked him too. Mario and Anna did everything together, and everyone knew that someday they would be married and live happily ever after like a storybook scene.

Well, once while I was sitting in the kitchen watching Mama cook, she told me, "You should have seen the look on Grandmama's face when I told her that I was pregnant with your brother, Marco, and wanted to get married!"

She said that my grandparents had been angry and disappointed with them. But since my Mama and Papa loved each other, they decided to run away from home together, get married, and start their new little family. And that's exactly what they did.

The downside to being in love and getting married while Mama was only sixteen and Papa was only seventeen was getting a place to stay, jobs, and money. Both, still in high school at the time, had to drop out to maintain their new family. Mama said, "It was okay because we both knew it would only be temporary until the baby was born, and then we'd go back and finish."

Yes, that was the plan. They moved into Papa's brother's basement, so they had a place to stay and a roof over the baby's head. Papa started working little odd jobs to bring in some money for food, diapers, and rent to give his brother every now and then. He finally landed a stable job as a janitor working the graveyard shift, and Mama worked as a cook during the day.

Well, this temporary arrangement wound up lasting about three years until the birth of my sister, Merissa. Mama would say that things were tight with just the three of them. While pregnant with Merissa, Mama's health kept her home in bed a lot of the time, and then after Merissa was born, Mama was laid off and had to stay home to watch Marco and Merissa. Things were not good at all, but they were able to get by. They had found their own place when Merissa was born, but Papa was finding it hard to keep money rolling in to cover the bills. He looked for a job during the day to help compensate for Mama not working but was unable to get anything and simply continued his night job as a janitor.

As luck would have it, and I do mean *bad* luck, Papa was laid off too. Times couldn't be any worse, and with no money coming in, two babies in the house, and more bills piling up, Papa had to take some extreme measures. One day, Papa decided to break into the corner store and steal some food and money out of the register. I was told that Papa had borrowed a gun from a friend but really didn't have any intentions of using it. Well, the store owner just happened to have a cot in the back room and was asleep when he heard banging and rustling sounds coming from the store. He grabbed a baseball bat, walked out of the back room, and cut the lights to the store. In utter surprise, Papa, without thinking, fired the gun in the direction of the store owner and killed him. It wasn't long before the police came to the scene of the crime, rushed into the store, and found Papa with all the merchandise and food he was trying to bring home scattered around him on the floor and the still-smoking gun clutched in his shaking hand. They ordered him to drop the gun. He'd had so many hopes and dreams, but nothing had worked out the way he had planned. After the third warning to drop the gun, instead of lowering the gun toward the floor, Papa raised it out of fear, and the police officers on the scene shot and fatally wounded him, thinking he was going to fire at them. Mama had never gotten the chance to tell him that she was pregnant again ... this time with me! Life after the death of my papa was never the same in our household.

Putting on My Own Shoes

Even though my life growing up had its setbacks, I was ready to strike out on my own and be a success. I wanted to make something out of myself. Merissa had learned a lot about how to be a perfect mother and housewife from being around Mama, but my plans were to be much more than the stereotypical married Latina. I wanted to travel the world, have lots of money, control my own destiny, and marry whoever I wanted, when I was ready. My choices in life were to be dictated by me, Maria Luisa Delgado, and me alone. I loved my Mama and my sister, but seeing how Mama struggled all my life, I wanted more. In fact, to be truthful, I needed more so I wouldn't end up like them ... I wanted excitement, challenge, and fulfillment in life. The sad part about my family was that most of the women were content having babies and taking care of their families. You know the old expression "barefoot and pregnant."

Growing up, I was always considered rather pretty with my long, flowing black hair. Mama would say, "You're my pretty doll, baby girl!" I would light up and smile from cheek to cheek every time she said that. Everyone liked me, especially the boys here in the barrio, but my brother made sure that nobody messed with his baby sister. In high school, I was determined not to make any mistakes with boys or anyone else who would prevent me from reaching my goals.

Every Sunday at Mass, I prayed that God would look out for me. I would say to God, "Don't let me be tempted by the boys. Don't allow me to go to parties and use drugs and drink alcohol. And, God, please, let me graduate, so I can leave the barrio."

It seemed that every time I left the church, a bunch of boys would start whistling and shouting at me to come and join them. But if they ever started to get a little touchy, Father Clements would step out, and they would run away. Father Clements would ask me if everything was okay, and I would say, "Yes, Father, I'm going to be all right." Father Clements once sat me down and shared with me a quote from Thomas Aquinas:

"There is within every soul a thirst for happiness and meaning." As a teenager, I had this thirst churning inside of me, and it seemed like it needed to erupt.

I made up my mind that since I was an honors student, the first step I needed to take to chart my course toward success was to go to college and get my degree in some major career field. I asked myself some direct and basic questions to help me determine my direction in life:

Who am I? Why am I here? And where am I going?

I began to realize that the answers to my questions would be found in college.

My best friend, Rita, also wanted to go to college, so the two of us spent a lot of time doing research and pulling information at the library. We didn't have a lot of many, so we limited filling out applications to only a couple colleges that would allow us to get away from home. Because we both were honors students with high test scores, it wasn't long before we both were getting invitations to visit many colleges with scholarships. Rita and I were so happy at this point; we felt that our dreams were about to come true. Well, after visiting several campuses and talking to a few guidance counselors, we selected a school not too far from home, since neither one of us had a car, but far enough to say we had left home. We felt that this school was exactly what we needed for now. After deciding on a college, we both set out to find summer jobs to make some extra money for school.

Rita started working at her parents' restaurant as a waitress, and I took on a job at a department store as a salesperson. We both set a goal to save as much money as we could, so we wouldn't struggle during the school year and must work after classes. It was great to have a plan, and this one was well underway. In fact, we both were working so hard and trying to get in as many hours as we could that we barely talked to one another anymore.

I was still helping at home, avoiding those boys with nothing on their minds but hanging out and getting high, and I kept myself busy. Of course, Father Clements seemed to always be stepping out of the chapel just in time to rouse the boys into going in the opposite direction from me.

Even though I tried to stay focused, there was a cute boy that caught my eye. He yelled from across the street as I passed by, "Hi! My name is Ricardo, but my friends call me Rico, Rico Juan Morales. What is yours? Look, I seen you around and wanted to ask you to go have a soda pop with me."

I don't know why—maybe because it was hot, and I had to practically run from the other boys—but his invite didn't seem half bad. In fact, I wanted to go and have some fun for a change of pace. Well, that first innocent date became the start of many more to come.

Rico and I hit it off great, and before we realized it, the Summer was coming to an end, and it was time for me to go off to college. Again, we weren't that far away, so Rico decided he would visit me as often as he could since he had a car. Rico would always pop up right when I needed him the most, and he understood my need to get away. We dated on the weekends so as not to disturb my study time during the week, but after the first year, it was getting harder for me to concentrate during the week without knowing what Rico was doing. I started daydreaming in class about getting married to Rico, living in a nice house with children, and having everything so perfect like a story out of a romance novel.

It had been weeks since I saw Rita, and then coming out of the dorm one day, I saw her sitting outside.

"Hey, girl, how are you?" I said joyfully.

Rita had a sad look on her face as she asked, "Have you heard from your family?"

"No, and I really haven't been trying to call them. Why?" I asked.

Looking very sad, Rita told me that my brother, Marco, had been shot and killed. Marco had drifted away with the wrong crowd, and we didn't speak to one another anymore. I really didn't feel any remorse for him, and I didn't plan to go back there for anything.

"Thank you," I said.

She asked abruptly, "When are you going home to check on things?"

To her surprise, I said, "I'm not! I have too much to do concentrating on my next big exam, and besides, Rico and I have special plans for the weekend."

I saw that she was shocked by my comment, so I reminded her, "We left the barrio to get away from things just like this, and I'm not going back for anything, ever!"

Rita stood up, shook her head, and quickly walked away from me without saying another word.

Dreams Do Come True

Things were moving along perfectly. I finished my second year, and Rico and I were so much in love that he asked, "Will you marry me?" I practically jumped in his arms with excitement, realizing that my dreams were about to all come true.

"Yes!" I said.

However, I still had this feeling that I really didn't know everything about Rico. For the last two years, we'd only truly spent time together on the weekends and on my school breaks, when he would take me to fancy places. But I really was in love with him. Besides, since I'd left the barrio, I felt that everything had been working out for me. I'd made the best choices, and marrying Rico only complemented how perfect my life was becoming. We decided to have a private, intimate marriage at the courthouse with a justice of the peace and spend some time in Vegas. Rico said he had a surprise planned for me once we got back.

When we returned, Rico drove me to this beautiful white house that looked like a mansion to me. I was in shock.

"Rico, honey, what is this?" I asked.

Rico quickly responded with his great smile, "This is your home, Mrs. Morales. My wife deserves the best!"

Though I was slightly curious, I nevertheless quickly hugged him and then shouted with appreciation as I quickly ran into our new home, far away from the barrio.

"Rico, it's beautiful! How are we able to afford such a house?" I asked.

Before I could continue to ask any more questions, his phone rang, and he excused himself to another room. Still amazed, I ran all through the house like a little child, opening and closing each door, admiring every inch of *my* house. About thirty minutes later, Rico came out of an office-like room and told me he had to run and take care of some business but that I should enjoy myself and he'd be back as soon as he could. I continued exploring the house, fixed myself something to eat out of the refrigerator, discovered our beautiful bedroom, and then fell asleep on the bed from exhaustion.

The next day, Rico asked me to just finish with my two-year degree, which I'd earned already, and not go back to school. He wanted me to be at home. I really didn't like the idea, since it was my goal to finish college, start my career, and then get married and have kids. I got angry at Rico and yelled, "I don't want to be a dropout like my parents! I set out to do this, and I'm going to!"

Rico had this disturbed look on his face but did not object. He only shook his head and walked away.

A few days later, Rico called and asked me to join him for lunch. At lunch he introduced me to Mr. George Henry Sebastian, who was dressed fancy. Mr. Sebastian asked if I would like a job at his firm. He said, "I'm looking for some real top-notch talent and heard how great you're doing in college."

I immediately came up with excuses why I couldn't take the job, so I could instead finish school, but then Rico said, "You have two years of college, and now here is your big chance. What are you waiting for?"

He was right, and I couldn't say a word against it. I turned to Mr. Sebastian and agreed. He shook my hand and let me know that he wanted me to start in about two weeks. Although a little sad, the next day I drove to campus and advised the admissions office that I wanted to petition to graduate with my two-year degree. A few weeks later, I received my degree by mail.

As time passed, I found myself getting more excited about starting the new job. Then one day the phone rang. It was the hospital confirming the lab results I had taken for the job. They were calling to tell me that I was pregnant. Again, I was filled with mixed emotions— excited that Rico and I were about to make all my dreams complete now with the arrival of a new baby but still worried that all of this could be happening way too soon.

When Rico got in that night, I sprang the good news on him, and he seemed more concerned about me going to work as planned and not telling anyone that we were going to have a baby.

He said, "Just go to work and act like you're just fine, and maybe you can get through without anyone noticing for a long time."

I decided he was just more concerned about me and would get more excited about our new arrival as the weeks went by.

"Okay," I said. "I'm heading up to bed now. Are you coming?"

Like usual, Rico shook his head no, went into his office without saying another word, and locked the door behind him. And once again, I retreated to our bedroom and fell asleep alone.

I started work and did well on the job. After five months, my baby bump was showing pretty good. Mr. Sebastian was quite pleased and offered to give me a raise to help with the baby. I was so excited and rushed home to tell Rico.

He yelled, "Why would he do this for you? You just started working there. What else are you doing there?"

I was stunned by his immediate outburst of anger. This was a side of him that I had never seen before. I did not like the tone of his accusations, and I yelled back, "What do you mean? At least you know where I work. You come and go as you please, have all this money, a fancy house, and cars, and I still don't know what you do or where you work!"

He turned his back and started to walk away from me, and in the heat of the argument and without thinking, I reached out to grab him. He then twirled around and shoved my arm away, knocking me sideways. In my condition, I lost my balance and fell down the long flight of stairs.

I woke up in the hospital a few hours later, feeling groggy, sore, and somewhat empty. As I started to regain consciousness, I noticed that Rico was nowhere to be seen, but my mama and my sister, Merissa, were in the room, sitting alongside my bed.

Without any greeting, I blurted out, "Why are you here? Where is my husband?"

Although they were visibly surprised by what I had just said, Mama mentioned that they had not seen Rico. She said, "The hospital called me directly since they had no way of reaching Rico. I guess they got my number from him before he had to leave."

I lay there wondering where he had to go that was more important than being there with me. But before I could get angry, I asked about the condition of my baby since it was quite a fall. Looking at the expressions on both Mama's and Merissa's faces, I could see that it wasn't good at all. They said the doctor would be in any moment to talk to me, and then Mama started to pray. I knew the news was not good. When we were growing up and Mama got bad news that she needed to share with the family, she would always start praying to the Virgin Mary and baby Jesus. Well, I didn't want baby Jesus; I wanted somebody to tell me about *my* baby. In disgust, I turned away from them.

About fifteen minutes later, after what seemed like an eternity of silence, the doctor and nurse both came in to check my vitals and give me the bad news I was already expecting.

The doctor said, "Mrs. Morales, in the fall, you suffered a fractured bone in your right arm, two cracked ribs, and a mild concussion. You will be fine; however, I'm sorry to tell you that because of the severe trauma in the fall, you lost the baby."

I immediately cried out in anguish and sobbed heavily. The doctor directed the nurse to give me a sedative to calm me down and put me to sleep. Faintly, I heard him ask my family to leave for now.

Who Are You

A few days passed, and Rico finally appeared. I saw by the expression on his face that he felt awfully bad about what had happened. I asked him where he'd been, and he finally shared with me what had seemed to be a mystery for several months now: Who was Rico?

As I lay there in shock, he told me, "I work for some very important people that pay me very well." He said that he had to go out of the country to pick up some packages that they wanted him to make sure were delivered for distribution.

"Packages? Packages for what kind of distribution, honey?" I asked in a naive tone.

Before he could answer, it hit me like a ton of bricks. The man that I had entrusted with my life and married was a drug dealer. I blurted it out without thinking.

He immediately said, "*Cállate!* [Shut up!] I'll explain it better when we get home. It isn't like you think. I'm not on the streets like those guys back in the barrio. Those guys work for me, so I'm protected from that kind of exposure and small-time stuff."

By the end of the week, Rico was able to take me home, but he demanded that I stay home for a while to heal and get better. I was still reeling from discovering who my husband really was, and I wanted to go back to work to keep my mind off losing the baby and our unresolved incident before the fall.

After a few days had passed, I needed to clear up the matter of why Rico had gotten so mad at me in the first place. He had never shown any signs of violence or such explosive anger before. *Did I push him to it?* I thought. *One minute, we were talking, and then I reached out and grabbed him. Now I see! I grabbed him, and he reacted! That makes sense now that I know what he actually does to make money. He felt threatened. I need to apologize to him and tell him it was all my fault.*

"Rico, can you come upstairs please?" I called.

I could hear that he was downstairs in the kitchen because of the rattling of pots and pans. Rico ran upstairs thinking that I was in pain or something, which I was, but I needed to really clear my mind.

I said, "We need to discuss what happened before I fell down the stairs."

Rico just stood by my bed staring at me with a look of both surprise and bewilderment. It seemed like minutes rolled by the only audible sound the ticking of the clock. Rico's face slowly began to look disturbed and angry just like before.

He said, "You need to rest and not think about anything right now. All you need is to get well! I have some pain pills that will work better than the mild stuff the doctor gave you. Okay?"

I didn't know whether he wanted to not talk about it at all or was really concerned about me. I looked up at him and said, "Okay, you know what's best for me, so we can talk in a few days about it."

Rico stepped out of the room and went downstairs. It took a long time, but he finally came back with my medication. He held a couple of pills in one hand and a glass of water in the other. He said, "Take these; you will feel much better!"

I took them and did not really think much about it. Several times a day, Rico would give me these pills, and each time I would fall asleep right away, as they worked quickly. Weeks seemed to pass by, and although I felt no pain, I also had no desire to get out of bed. *By now, Mr. Sebastian has replaced me, and I have no job*, I thought.

Rico was spending more and more time away from the house, and when he was home, I always seemed to hear the voices of several men downstairs talking business with him. Yes, Rico was in his own world, dealing drugs I guess, but I wasn't about to take the chance of bringing that up again.

49

Eventually Rico stopped giving me any medication. I was beginning to feel really strange. I was shaking all over, my mouth stayed dry, and all I wanted was my pills. Maybe due to my current state of mind, I threatened Rico and told him,

"We need to talk now about what's going on in the house. Who are all these people? Are you bringing drugs in here?"

Rico started to yell back at me in Spanish but then just turned around and abruptly walked out of the room, slamming the door behind him.

I was so upset that I yelled through the closed door, "Don't you walk out on me while I am talking to you!"

I heard him stomp down the stairs and slam the front door, and then there was only dead silence. I guess I was having a brain overload, as I began to feel light-headed and in dire need of some medication.

Why did I chase him away? I need him to help me, and there is no one else, I thought. I started to panic and get anxious.

The pain was unbearable now. I knew that Rico kept the pills somewhere downstairs in his private office, so I managed to pull myself up out of bed. Clutching tightly to the bannister and taking one step at a time, ever so carefully, I gradually and slowly eased myself downstairs. I had been in Rico's private office only once before rather briefly, and I had felt like I shouldn't be in there then. It was his *private* office because that was how he'd set the limits within the house in the beginning. Well, I didn't care right now, because I needed those pills. The door was unlocked, so I walked in, and my eyes quickly focused on his desk.

"They have to be in here," I said quite loudly.

I'm not sure what I was really feeling at the time. It definitely wasn't the same kind of pain I had experienced from the accident, but something was seriously going on in my body. The room was spinning, but before I fainted or lost consciousness, I was able to find a couple of bottles of pills. I practically ripped the lid off of one of the bottles. These pills looked different from the ones Rico had given me before, but I didn't care—I needed something immediately. I poured several pills into my hand. I didn't count how many and quickly popped them in my mouth. I looked around and realized that I would not be able to make it to the kitchen and then back upstairs to my bedroom, so I conveniently took a shot from one of Rico's bottles of liquor to help the pills go down. Afterward, I crawled my way back upstairs and into bed. Before I passed out again, I felt everything fade away from my senses as a wonderful, euphoric feeling took over.

This is the best I've felt ever, I thought and then closed my eyes.

In the still of the night, I heard the front door open and close. I thought, *Oh, Rico must be back! I need to tell him I'm sorry for yelling at him.* So many things danced around in my head, so many questions I needed to talk to Rico about, but before I could do anything, I passed out again.

Downstairs, Rico was having his own private celebration. He grabbed his bottle of tequila, poured a rather large glassful, and drank it down in almost one swallow. He poured another glass and noticed his desk drawer pulled slightly open. He then noticed a pill bottle right on top of some papers and a few other items out of place. Rico immediately looked up at the ceiling as though he was looking into the bedroom to see Maria. He again emptied his glass and started to laugh.

"I must be imagining things! There's no way she could have come down here, found these pills, and taken them. No way!" Rico said to himself and again laughed at the thought.

Rico turned around and unlocked his file cabinet. In the bottom drawer was a box filled with empty pill bottles and behind that another box. On the box was a yellow warning label and the name Fentanyl.

Rico packaged up all the pills, and then Juan and Carlos, Rico's main boys, knocked on the door. Rico opened the door and handed them the packages.

"Homeys, this is the stuff that will make us some more dough and set us up big-time back on the streets. They call it 'Jackpot,' and we gonna hit it big. Get these circulated as quickly as possible," Rico said as he slapped Carlos on his shoulder. With a big grin on his face, Rico closed the door and returned to his bottle of tequila.

"*Salud!* Life is really good!" Rico said as he emptied the bottle and headed up to bed.

A few days went by, and because of the new product, Rico's popularity and business were booming. There was so much excitement and money rolling in that he failed to notice the change in Maria. What Rico also failed to see the night he discovered the pill bottle in the wrong place was that one was actually missing. Maria had shoved one bottle in her gown pocket and had been taking the pills several times a day. By the time Rico did become aware of his wife and her condition, she was already addicted to the drug and on a fast-paced downward spiral. The great feelings she'd experienced days ago now were slowly eating away at her inner soul.

Not Exactly in the Plan

As tears rolled down my face, I thought, *How could I have been so stupid as to fall for this? How could I have been so blinded by love that I did not see the consequences? I did this to myself!*

I had progressed in my drug habit, mixing the pills with alcohol, going day to day with not a care in the world except for my habit. Rico hardly ever came home anymore because he couldn't stand what I had become, barricading myself in my room and not wanting help from anyone, just more drugs.

There was nothing in Rico's office anymore. He had removed the temptation, but the damage was already done. In fact, Rico had realized that he could not afford me sneaking into his product and getting high whenever I felt like it. I guess he decided to move it all to his warehouse and leave nothing more in the house that could cause any more trouble. Or so he thought!

"I need something!" I said to myself as I stumbled to the front door, not caring what I looked like and trying to find someone to help me with a fix.

As I opened the door, my mama and Merissa were standing there getting ready to knock. Surprise! After a long period of worrying and not knowing what was going on with me since I'd left the hospital, they'd decided to get my address from the hospital admittance office since they had no way of contacting me directly. They both were shocked to see the state I was in: drunk, high, and talking abusively toward them. You see, I was so angry with myself that I did not care about anyone else or their feelings.

Mama kept saying to me over and over again, "Maria, we need to pray that Jesus delivers you from these drugs and that alcohol. Jesus will heal you!"

A few moments later, I got so fed up with all the lecturing that I blew up and started cursing at Mama and Merissa. While yelling, I launched my bottle at them and while shaking my fist said, "Never come back here, and take that religious stuff back home with you. I don't want or need it here! All I need is right here in my house with my husband." They hurriedly ran out the door, both crying and speaking in Spanish.

As my condition worsened, Rico quickly tired of my using and drinking all day long. In fact, it was not long before Rico decided that I was becoming more trouble for him. There was no love anymore, and I had definitely become quite a burden for Rico and trouble for the business.

In a state of rage, Rico told me, "I am sick and tired of you. You need to get out of my house now, this minute!"

I couldn't believe what I was hearing. I tried to fight him, but I was too high to really know what was happening to me. Rico and his friends literally grabbed me and a small suitcase, which they had already packed for me, and threw me out of my own house!

So here I am. Abandoned on the street... cold, hungry, alone, and confused. What happened to my storybook life? What happened to all the plans and dreams I had for fulfilling my road to success? Was it all only a fantasy? Why does my story have to be written as a rags-to-riches-to-rags story instead of a happy-ending tale? What do I do now? I need help but don't know where to go or who to turn to!

Reflective Key Verse

> Be sober; be vigilant; because your adversary the devil
> walks about like a roaring lion, seeking whom he may
> devour.
>
> —1 Peter 5:8

Spiritual Moment

There are moments in life that one tends to never forget. Peter, one of the twelve disciples and part of Jesus' inner circle, had his highs and lows, and one of his lows occurred when he was not sober minded and watchful. Peter discovered that, just like many of us, he also could fall easy prey under the intense attack of Satan. When Jesus was arrested in the garden of Gethsemane, Peter followed them to the high priest's house where he denied that he knew Jesus. Peter had not been thinking soberly and had not been watchful, even in a literal sense, and shortly afterward was caught in the Devil's trap. And we can see his memory at work as he recalled that sad time.

Life and circumstances resemble in part the strategic maneuvers of the Devil. He uses camouflage to keep his tactics undetectable until it is too late or right upon you. In our reflective key verse, Peter suggests that we should have a certain attitude at all times. Christians are to be sober and alert. Sobriety refers to our way of thinking, and alertness describes our concern about possible dangers.

Life Challenge

If a Christian is marked by sobriety and alertness, he or she will not fall, no matter how fierce the Devil's opposition becomes. Christians are in a war, and a war situation demands keeping a clear head and looking for potential attacks.

We would expect a soldier on guard duty to be serious as well as alert. And we are always on guard duty, in a sense, because we have to protect ourselves from the Enemy of our souls.

A Christian knows that the Devil can be in only one place at a time, but the believer cannot tell who the Devil will target next. Therefore realistic Christians will always be ready because they know that the Devil could attack at any moment. Everything may look splendid for a precious moment, but never become too complacent; he is ready to pounce like the roaring lion he resembles.

CHAPTER 4

Pastor Brown's Story: We All Fall Down—What's Next?

Lord, how they have increased who trouble me! Many are they who rise up against me. Many are they who say of me, There is no help for him in God. But You, O Lord, are a shield for me; My glory and the One who lifts up of my head. I cried to the Lord with my voice, and He heard me from His Holy hill.

—Psalm 3:1–4

Where Are Those Happy Days

"Good Morning, Reverend. Praise the Lord! What a blessing to be in the land of the living. How are you doing?" says Mother Josephine King, the Church Mother here at Glory Gate Holiness Missionary Baptist Church.

I look up from my study and reply, "Mother, it certainly is!"

But in my heart, I find it difficult to believe the words. In my heart, I can hear, "I'm not really fine at all, and if you were me, you wouldn't be either." All the while I sit here trying not to look at the picture on the wall directly behind Mother King. It's a picture of my father, the late Reverend Cleophus Jackson Brown. Every time I look at that picture, I can hear my dad's voice, stern and abrupt, telling me, "Son, God will help you along the way." I think God must be helping someone in worse shape than me because I'm all alone here.

I'm having one of those days that seems like it will never end. In fact, I normally dread facing day after miserable day caught up in this meaningless cycle of "what next?" I am too filled with pride to allow anyone to know that I am virtually miserable on the inside. The sad part about it all is that I am such a great actor that no one suspects that it all is a sham! My days are determined by what circumstances I encounter. If things go well, I have a great day, but if not, I feel like giving up.

Today started bad and hasn't changed one bit. In fact, maybe it's worse because I've had to bottle up all my troubles. I feel like a boat out in the middle of the ocean, tossed back and forth by the unpredictable storms that seem to show up all the time now. I have no rudder, no sense of direction, and no control over standing strong. But you know how it is. I'm a preacher, a man of God who walks by faith and not by sight—or at least, I'm supposed to be able to do that. Oh, it may be a "blessed" day for you, but you aren't having the kind of day that I'm having. Actually, today is no different from yesterday and the day before that and the day before that. How do I begin to recall when all these bad days started? It seems to me that my troubles resemble the effect of a snowy avalanche in some mountainous area. It started off as something small, but now that it's picked up momentum, it's enormous and out of control. Don't get me wrong: I still love God. I still work just as hard as ever. I still meditate both day and night on His Word. I still help the people in the community, and I still sacrifice my time. But it seems like it's never enough. No one's ever satisfied. Even when I give my best, it just isn't enough for some folk. I honestly feel that it is not a blessing to be in the land of the living if I have to face turmoil each and every day. Why me? I've been lied to, talked about, mistreated, scorned, and knocked almost to the ground. I know it sounds like that song Vickie Winans sings: "As long as I got King Jesus, I don't need nobody else." Well, where is my King Jesus when I need Him the most? And I sure don't have anybody else to whom I'd even care to try to explain how I feel and what I'm dealing with inside.

"Okay, King Jesus, I need You. Anytime now would work for me just fine!" I say a few times a day. I even pause expecting to hear a loud baritone voice like that of James Earl Jones or the guy from the Allstate commercial bellowing out from heaven. You've heard them speak on TV, and their voices, whether seen or unseen, command your attention. That's what I expect to hear from God, something like, "Clarence, don't worry about a thing!"

And I would answer, "Lord, I knew I could count on You."

And then in return in a stern but confidence-building voice, God would say, "You're in good hands, My son."

You know, some days I wonder if my daddy made a mistake turning the church over to me. I spend the days here in my office miserable, I go home to my family and make them miserable, and it just seems that I'm not cut out to walk in my daddy's shoes. Yes, I may look like him, but that's where it stops I think. I don't ever recall my daddy coming home from church or a business meeting at the church all mad and irritated from things not going as planned or bumping heads with the deacon board or worrying about getting the money to pay all the bills, fix stuff, and just keep the church operating. Maybe I missed it or he hid it well, but I don't remember my daddy with such a weight on his shoulders as I seem to be bearing now.

The Little Preacher's Kid (PK)

Momma would yell up the stairs, "Clarence, don't forget to brush your teeth. And don't forget to put your tie on. And you need to hurry up and not make your daddy late."

Momma always let me put on my little white shirt, black suit, shiny shoes, and tie so I looked just like my daddy, the Reverend Cleophus Jackson Brown. I loved my folks. They were the greatest parents a child could ever have. Momma stayed at home; did the housework; raised me and my two sisters, Hattie and Martha; and made sure Daddy had what he needed every day. Momma actually stayed away from the church during the week but never missed a Sunday there to support Daddy. Momma never shouted or jumped up out of her seat like most of the people. She just calmly sat there with eyes and ears alert to every word my daddy said and every action he made. After the service, we'd walk home, and Momma would pat Daddy on his back and tell him, "You did wonderful again today, as always!"

Daddy would just smile and nod his head. He always told me that he didn't get too excited about what the congregation said to him after the service, things like, "Rev, you did real good today!" or "Pastor, you preached today!"

Daddy would say, "If I preached that good, then those folks better start listening to what I say and do it!" Then he'd laugh and say, "But I guess I did all right, Son!"

Daddy once told me that he had been serving as a deacon at the church when the old Reverend Jenkins became sick and later passed away. The church then voted my daddy in as pastor because he was outspoken and carried himself well. Daddy said, "They just took a shine to me, and they will do the same for you."

I loved going to church with my daddy because it was man time. Daddy would let me go with him to church meetings, sit in his office, read his big Bible, and sometimes even sit in the pulpit with him. I'd go back home in the evening and show my sisters how I would pastor the church like Daddy, practice preaching with all his same facial and hand expressions and slaying my congregation of two in the Spirit, just like Daddy did his congregation on Sundays. I'd stand on an old milk crate, shake my fist, and preach like Daddy. My sisters, Hattie and Martha, would pretend they had tambourines and sing like the choir. Hattie would jump up during my minisermon every now and then to shout "Hallelujah! Preach on, preacher, preach!" just like old Mother Haley would say in church.

Every so often, Mrs. Peters, our neighbor, would walk up the dirt road toward town, stop, and say, "Boy, you sounding and looking just like your daddy each and every day. One day, you gonna be the pastor of our church just like your daddy."

I'd poke out my chest and confidently say, "Thank you, ma'am!"

If I knew then what I know now, I would have played something else. Yet because I loved my daddy and the way he was, I wanted to grow up and be just like him.

There were always people at our little house for something. The deacon board would come over and talk to Daddy about the people. The trustee board would come to talk about the money. The Mothers' Board would talk to Daddy about the improper dress attire of some of the ladies, and the usher board would talk to Daddy about getting more fans and placing stuff in the bulletins so people would wait outside during prayer and Scripture reading and not just barge in. Even members of the church would come over and bare their souls to Daddy asking for prayer and a little money to get them by until the first of the month. All of this and never once did I see Daddy get mad, curse, or complain. He just shook his head and let everyone know that it would be all right.

Glory Gate Holiness Missionary Baptist Church has been around since 1962. This old country church has a lot of history and sentimental memories for most of the folk in the community. The leadership prefers to repair problems that occur with the church, but with the shape it's in, they should consider tearing it down and rebuilding it. Nice idea, but where would we get the money?

One day, in the deep of winter, while Daddy was still the pastor, the furnace went out with a large bang that reverberated through the building. I know this because our little house was right next door to the church. The choir was rehearsing, and the deacons were meeting with Daddy about some church stuff when the explosion echoed through the church.

I ran over to find my daddy and see what had happened. My daddy simply turned to the chairman of deacons and said, "Sounds like the furnace done played out, and we will need a new one. That old thing has probably been here since the church was built in 1962; it was due to break down"

With that, Deacon Mac looked at Daddy, dropped his head, and said, "We don't really have the money, but the Lord will make a way, right, Reverend?"

Daddy just smiled and said, "Right, Deac!"

And don't you know, by Sunday we had heat and a new furnace working in the church. Daddy never worried about a thing. That's just the way he handled business, always very calm like there was never a problem at all.

So when Daddy got real sick and couldn't preach anymore, the deacons and the people came to him and asked, "What should we do?" From his sickbed, Daddy calmly said, "My boy is ready! Tell the people to give him a chance. He knows all he needs to know about running this church like I have done. He will make an excellent choice for you." I heard all these fine comments and let them go to my head, thinking I could actually run the church and the people. That was my first mistake of the pastorate.

A week later, the church held a business meeting with the entire congregation and voted me in as the next pastor of Glory Gate Holiness Missionary Baptist Church. Daddy and Momma were a part of that vote. The church was full, and the decision was unanimous. You should have seen the way my daddy's face lit up when the final decision was made. This was Daddy's last formal act as pastor. A few days later, Daddy died. Momma told me that he had been sickly for a while but had kept it to himself. He didn't get a chance to install me in as pastor, but Momma blessed me with his Bible. I'm so happy that Momma let me have Daddy's Bible. Daddy never went anywhere without his Bible tucked under his arm. It was tattered from years of wear and tear; in fact, Daddy told me that he had gotten this Bible from his daddy, who was also a preacher. I guess you can say that I inherited more than just the Bible but also the family legacy of preachers.

I'm the Pastor—Now What?

Back in the present, I sit in my daddy's chair behind his desk in his church office and pray that I can fill his shoes and carry on the mission that has been passed down to me. "Okay, Lord, show me the way!" I say. "Lord, don't let me be a disappointment; teach me to be just like my daddy, Pastor Cleophus Brown!"

It's amazing; although I grew up a PK, pretended to be a preacher on many occasions, and even held pretend church in the yard with my sisters, nothing could have prepared me for what I now faced as pastor. You can observe many things in life and really not have a clue until you have to handle the situation yourself. My daddy made this look pretty charming and pleasurable, but I seem to be missing out on the good times of leading a congregation of God's people. I think, *God, You do have a sense of humor, because things surely can't get any worse, and You continue to leave me stranded.*

I have to pinch myself. As I look over at Daddy's picture, I swear I hear the picture tell me, "Son, it's only a test. Hang in there! God is preparing you for a greater service." Preparing me for a greater service than pastoring a church? I wonder what that could be.

I say, "Okay, Lord! I guess I've faced the worse, so I'm ready! I think?"

You remember that old Morton Salt slogan that used to be on TV? Of course you don't see it much anymore, because folks are concerned about their health, reducing their salt intake to prevent high blood pressure and other health-related issues. But back in the day, the commercial would come on with a little girl wearing a yellow raincoat and holding an umbrella, and then the slogan would flash: "When it rains, it pours." Today, I need *my* raincoat and umbrella because it's definitely pouring down hard on me.

I slog through the rest of the day and head home, knowing the whole thing will start over the next day. First thing the next morning, as I rush out the door without breakfast (as usual), my wife, Rebecca, says, "Honey, don't forget to go to Robbie's Little League game today at two, and then after that, you have to run to the concert hall because Karen wants you to be at her first recital."

I loved being a family man. I used to spend practically every day with my family. My wife and I would get up early, pray together, have breakfast and coffee, read certain Bible passages to one another, walk the kids to the bus stop or drop them off at school, go to work, and then come home in the evening to share our daily experiences at the dinner table together, as a family. I never missed any school meetings, our kids' extracurricular activities, or weekend fun days just going to the park or anywhere else nice we could go as a family. I used to be my son's Little League coach. I made sure I sat and helped both kids with their homework and listened to Karen as she practiced her violin and smoothed out every sour note. I used to call Rebecca and see how her day was going and then surprise her by coming home early with a nice meal for the family. We were kind of like a mini–Huxtable family, just like *The Cosby Show*. We did everything as a loving family, like in the Bible. We laughed together, played together, ate meals together, discussed our days together, and like *The Cosby Show*, pretty much did everything together in the public eye. Well, Cliff and Clair Huxtable didn't have to worry about pastoring a church full of childish individuals.

But now I rush out of my home, which I neglect because the church comes first. I pull up to the church, and before I've finished parking, out comes somebody needing something. This always happens; if it isn't one of the deacons or trustees, then it's one of the other staff members.

"Pastor, you got a minute?" asks Deacon Harris.

I think, *A minute? I can't even get into the church before I'm bombarded.* Out loud I say, "Yes, Deacon Harris, I'll be right in!"

As I continue to sit for just a moment, an urge comes over me to just shift the car in reverse and go home. Just for a moment. Then reality knocks at the window; it's Sister Shirley. "Pastor, we need to talk!"

I guess I'd just better turn the car off and force myself into another day at the church, another day full of anxiety, strife, and "Oh my goodness, what will we do now?" Maybe that's too sarcastic, but every day, it's the same routine: somebody needs me to do something for them. I just pray that one of these days, some of these grown folks will start acting like they know what they are supposed to do and stop adding to my already-heavy load of burdens. If you want my opinion, the deacons have decided to all take a spiritual break and leave everything for me to handle. Well, it seems that way 'cause I know each one of them and their roles, and yes, I am still learning all of mine, but I'm almost positive some of the decisions and issues that come to me could easily be resolved by them.

As I enter my office and place my briefcase down, in comes Sister Shirley. "Pastor Brown, Pastor Brown! Lord, have mercy; we have to talk right now! I don't know if you've heard the news yet?"

I look up at her and ask her to calm down and have a seat. Then in the back of my mind I think, *Here we go again!* Just another day at the office. What could be so bad this time?

Trouble That Hits Hard

Feeling much like King David from the Holy Bible. You do remember that David, don't you, the man described in the Bible as "a man after

God's own heart" in Acts 13:22. He had some trouble come his way too.

Much of King David's story is found in 2 Samuel 13:30–18:33. As a shepherd boy anointed by the Prophet Samuel to be the next king, David killed the Philistine giant Goliath to save his people. He became king after Saul and showed courage, bravery, and great leadership on many occasions as a warrior king. He regained control of Jerusalem, making it the capital of the Israelites and then brought back the Ark of the Covenant. All of this came from the same David who committed adultery with Bathsheba; had her husband, Uriah, murdered; and then took her as his very own wife. Then this David was driven out from his palace, from the royal city, from the holy city, by his rebellious son Absalom, who formed a conspiracy against him to take away not only his crown but also his life. And so David was disgraced by the rebellion of his very own son Absalom. I'll finish the story later.

My Bible tells me that even though I will have trouble, I need to trust in God. So feeling defeated, I think, *Okay, God, what do I do now? At times it feels like both my family and the church are rebelling against me and like you've turned your back on me. What's the use?*

I suddenly snap away from my spiritual walk through the Bible and realize that I've forgotten about Sister Shirley sitting here waiting to talk to me.

"Sister Shirley! Hi! What's going on?" I ask.

"Pastor, as your church treasurer, I need to inform you that the church budget is in the red. We need a new roof, and the congregation would like a new air-conditioning unit put in the sanctuary 'cause the old one is not keeping it cool in there. And, Pastor, we need to cut your salary in order to continue to pay the bills. I'm sorry to be the bearer of this news, but you just need to know. Do you have any ideas?" She looks at me as though she is waiting for some miraculous, save-the-day stroke of wisdom to drop out of the sky into my head and pour out of my mouth.

Actually, I sit there in shock with only the last statement ringing in my head—cut my salary? "Ummm, let me pray about it and get back to you!" I've gotten quite good at saying that so folks won't think I don't know what I'm doing or what to say, even though, to be honest, I don't. As Sister Shirley gets up and leaves, in walks another, and I still haven't had my first cup of coffee yet. All I can think about is an endless parade of trouble.

"Deacon Harris, what can I do for you, sir?" I ask.

"Pastor, I told you I needed to talk to you, before that ole Sister Shirley came running in here blabbing her mouth. I know she told you about the financial problems, and we'll talk about that more later on. I scheduled a meeting for us with the bank to see about another loan."

I think, *Another loan?*

"Oh, and we have a meeting later with the association CPA. He needs to audit the books, and there's no one else available to be with him but you and me. That's right after lunch, but it shouldn't take long. Okay?"

"Sure, that will be fine!"

It wouldn't be, but what else was I going to say. Just be humble and smile. That's the role I must play just to get through the day. I receive yet another knock on the door, and one of the other deacons comes in to advise me that I need to go down to the hospital to make my morning visit and then over to the Sunrise Adult Living Home and then meet with the Jones family to help them arrange for their mom's funeral service. "And don't forget Mother King wants you to come by and pray for her grandchildren who won't come to church. Okay, Pastor?" says Deacon Jones.

Meeting after meeting, visit after visit, and what time is it anyway? Six o'clock! I forgot to turn my phone back on after all the meetings. When I finally power it up, I have about one hundred missed calls, all from my wife. Okay, maybe that's a slight exaggeration, but I have missed another opportunity to see my son play, I've missed my daughter's first recital, and it looks like I'm going to miss family dinner again! I hope there's room in the doghouse tonight because that's where I'm headed. And to be honest, I don't know what good I've done at all today. I'm not sure if we'll get the loan to rescue us from our debt and get the roof fixed. I'm not sure if I lifted anyone's spirits at the hospital or nursing home or the mortuary. I had better call home and let Rebecca know that I'm running late again. As I reach to dial home, in pops Deacon Harris.

"Pastor, I'm so glad I caught you! We need to announce to the staff and leadership that we are calling a special meeting to address this financial mess we're in."

Reluctantly, I nod, knowing that at the end of the day all fingers will be pointed at me. Every time things don't go the way everyone wants them to go, it's my fault: "Pastor, what are *you* going to do? Your daddy, the Reverend Brown, would never have let this happen!"

I find myself praying, "Lord, hold my peace!"

As I enter the house that night, it's very quiet, and the lights are dimmed. There's no dinner on the dining room table; it will be in the refrigerator, cold by now. Kids are asleep. My wife is in our bedroom with the door closed. I knock but get no response. I remember I forgot to call home.

"Man, I'm in the doghouse again!" I say as I slowly walk back downstairs and prepare for bed on the sofa.

The next day—after a rough night on the couch and the cold shoulder and silent treatment from the family—they all leave the house while I'm still struggling to get off the couch. I get myself ready, drive to church, and the cycle continues as it does every day in the life of Reverend Clarence Brown, pastor of Glory Gate Holiness Missionary Baptist Church. Today is the same and yesterday and the day before that. More meetings unscheduled and scheduled. More issues to resolve or pray about. More blame games! And in the middle of it all, I stand! This cross is getting too heavy to bear.

"Lord, what do You want me to do?" I ask. "I can't seem to do anything to make anyone happy. The more I try to be all things to all people, I fall short with someone."

I sigh and leave my office for the special meeting, which, I must admit, goes south really quick. Neither my mom nor my wife comes. I guess Rebecca is still mad at me. Maybe I should call and apologize for yesterday. I have to explain to her what's going on. The leadership has decided that even though they think I'm wonderful and a great preacher, some things around the church have to change for the better or else they will vote me out. I guess my trial period is about to expire, and the happy times are about to end. Can things get any worse?

As I really start to feel depressed, the church secretary rushes in to let me know that my mom has been rushed to the hospital after having a heart attack. By the time I make it there, she is gone. I look at Rebecca, and she just shakes her head, saying, "You're late again! I hope they decide to ask someone who will be on time to conduct the funeral service."

Here I go again, feeling like David! Oh yes, let's go back to where I left off in that story:

King David was now in imminent and ever-increasing danger; the plot by his son Absalom against him was set and well orchestrated. Absalom's loyal rebels had chased David from the royal city and were ready to ensure the ruin of the now-dethroned king. Can you imagine your own son, your own blood, the child you raised, becoming the man that wants you destroyed? I feel like David, isolated and so alone, in a situation that is draining me and causing me to want to flee and escape it all. How did things grow so out of control so quickly? Christian folk, church people that I love and have dedicated my life to, all seem to have raised up in revolt against me, and now I don't even have my family to help gird me up. As I leave the hospital, a voice in my head keeps saying, "*Run!*"

When I was in school, I didn't have a lot of friends, because they called me "church boy" and made fun of me for not hanging out, playing sports, or dating like some of the other boys. One summer, before I graduated, Daddy allowed me to go to camp, part of the men's retreat at church. We had our own cabins for our group of about fifty or so boys, and we did a lot of activities, including prayer and group studies, with a few hours of extracurricular activities.

I had never gone camping or fishing or done any of the competitive activities they allowed us to do to break the monotony of just church activities. I guess they wanted us to have fun and bond in a variety of ways. One boy there was not a part of our church. As I heard later, his grandfather had given him a choice to either go on the retreat with the church or go behind bars at the juvenile detention center because he was getting out of hand—stealing, fighting, and causing a lot of trouble. His name was Raymond, "Ray" for short.

The camp counselors placed us in groups for certain exercises and events. On one occasion, Ray and I were paired up for the day, and by the end of the day, we had talked and gotten to know one another pretty well. He did not really care for the praying, the Bible studying, or singing of church hymns. I could tell that it was different for him but calming.

Ray shared with me that his mother had given him up when he was little to an adoption agency because she was too young to handle caring for him without a man in the picture, the man having left once she told him she was pregnant, and she feared the reprisal from her parents. So he spent most of his youth in and out of foster homes. He was already twelve years old when his grandparents finally found him and adopted him. His grandparents told him that his mom had died from a drug overdose. They said they had not known about Ray until she'd told them right before the night of her accident. Ray said that he'd been filled with so many mixed emotions: happy to be in a real home with his own grandparents but saddened that he'd never gotten a chance to know his mom.

Ray was pretty much on his own most of his youthful life and did what he wanted behind his grandparents' backs. He had been expelled from school for fighting and cutting classes and had been in and out of juvenile hall for vandalizing property and stealing. Ray oftentimes was caught smoking weed and drinking alcohol in the alley. His grandparents' patience was wearing thin, and that was when they gave him an option to either come here to camp or off to jail and out of their home. I could see the anger raging in his eyes, but from his story, I knew that this was the best choice he could have ever made. I think God wanted me to help him to change for the better. We left camp and promised to see one another and continue our friendship, and then three weeks later, I heard that Ray had attempted an armed robbery. He was tried as an adult since he was almost eighteen years old, found guilty, and sent to jail. I guess that should have been my first clue that I would be a failure to those I thought I was helping.

Choices to Live By

I'm losing all interest in being at the church anymore. I'm scared someone will had me a pink slip and say, "Pastor, we appreciate what you've done for the church; however, your services are no longer needed." And if that doesn't happen, I still have the never-ending parade of issues marching into my office and landing on my already-overburdened shoulders. So I stay home for a few days. Every morning, Deacon Harris calls and asks if I'm coming in, and I pretend to be sick. Rebecca decides to take the kids and go live with her parents after my mom's funeral. She tell me that once I've decided that they are important to me, they will come back.

"Wow, I'm sinking fast, Jesus! It's getting harder to keep my eyes on you and deal with all these things happening to me. I'm beginning to feel like Job—being slain each and every day. But I don't know who to trust."

A week after my mom's funeral, I run into Ray. I haven't seen him since camp, and I am so surprised to see him out of jail. We decide to grab a drink.

"Ray, how are you?" I ask.

Ray looks different and seems to have that old, mean look he had when I first met him at camp.

"Church boy! Man, it's been a minute since I last saw you. You must be running the church by now!" he says sarcastically, not realizing how close to the truth he really is.

"Yes, I pastor my father's church now!" I say.

Looking at me, Ray says, "Hey, church boy, you don't look too happy about it. What's up? Last time we were together, all you talked about was the church, the Bible, praying, and your God. We've sat here at this table, and you haven't mentioned any of those things once. You haven't talked about your parents or your family or your job, Mr. Reverend Dr. Pastor Church Boy! What's going on? Isn't this when you're supposed to tell me that this booze is evil and I need to stop drinking and whatever else you may think I'm doing! You know, pull out that Bible you carried around in camp all the time and share some Jesus with me?"

I tell Ray about my mom recently dying, being rejected by my family for spending too much time at church and not enough time at home, and to beat all, the church trying to get rid of me! Before I can continue my sad discourse, the bartender comes around and asks if I want anything to drink other than water.

"Yes, give me what he has!" I say, pointing to Ray.

Ray almost chokes on his drink as he swallows it down and asks for another. "You must be going through something, man! Let's just relax and chill tonight and we can talk about it tomorrow. You don't preach to me, and I won't question you! Deal?" Ray has a somewhat-puzzling look on his face.

"Deal," I say.

The next day, I wake up much later than usual and am still a little hungover from last night. Instead of my usual routine of going to the church and attending all the meetings that really don't do anything for anybody, I call Ray and set up plans to meet with him down at the Starbucks downtown for lunch. I feel the need to really connect with someone. I have all these mixed emotions, and I'm also curious about Ray's life and if he has changed from his troublesome past. Actually, I don't even know why I want to know; I mostly just like having someone who is not demanding anything of me.

Ray and I meet, and he shares about his prison time and why he committed the robbery, but he also tells me that since he's been out, things have gone perfectly for him.

"Church boy, I have a few business arrangements with certain people, which has allowed me to hook up people with what we call small-business loans," says Ray.

I'm happy that Ray has apparently become successful since he left jail. Many times I have spoken to ex-cons who couldn't find a decent job after being released from prison because nobody wanted to hire them. Lawmakers put them in jail, say that they have "reformed" them, and place them back in society to make a new lease on life—only for us to turn our backs on them and refuse to give them a chance to prove that they have changed their ways and can be a productive part of society now that they have the right tools.

I am also intrigued that Ray might be able to help me with a loan for the church, which would hopefully save my job and marriage. I think that maybe it is a good thing that I ran into Ray and we had those drinks together. Maybe now he can help me, and I can get myself out of this pitiful state I'm in.

"I need a big favor!" I say with a sense of urgency in my voice. "The church needs a loan in order to pay some debts, get the roof fixed, and take care of some other issues. We've been turned down by the bank, and I don't know where else to go."

"Church boy, look here—for you, not a problem! How much do you need? Come by and see me later at the pool hall, and we can work out the terms," Ray says.

I am so happy that he will bail us out of our problems that I miss the warning signs and the still voice of God speaking into my spirit, telling me to trust Him and He will direct my path. I am so blinded by the offer that I don't realize that there could be a major cost that is not worth the amount of the loan. I actually forget about God. I run away from trusting and believing in the power of prayer. I am so driven I forget to count the cost. Perils and frights should drive us to God, not away from him.

Grabbing my phone, I immediately call Deacon Harris and Sister Shirley and ask them to meet me in my office within the next hour. All the while, I hear a tiny voice repeatedly saying, "Trust Me!" Although I know where it is coming from, I decide to shut it out. Instead of praying and believing that God is about to turn around my situation and the church's situation, all I can see are the insurmountable obstacles being built up against me.

"Sorry, God, this is our way out and my way back into the love of my family and church. I'm about to become the hero! I'm about to show them that I'm just as capable as my father was," I say.

In my office, I look at the financial report and what we requested from the bank to fulfill our needs. After reviewing the report and ledger, I look up and say to Deacon Harris and Sister Shirley, "Our problems are solved. We can stop begging the bank for a handout. I will have all we need soon, and I will get us out of this mess we're in!"

"But how?" Deacon Harris asks with a look of disbelief.

With a wide smile on my face, I say, "I have some connections that will come to our rescue."

I sit there and see their faces light up like neon lights on Broadway, and a glimmer of confidence and pride overcomes me. I haven't even told Ray how much I need, and I don't know if he will be willing to give me that much, but I am already patting myself on the back.

That evening, I meet with Ray at the pool hall. He has two big guys in the office with him. They stare me down with their arms crossed. I feel a little uncomfortable, but really my only concern is getting the money for the church.

"Thanks for offering to help me out," I tell Ray. "I need about $50,000, and all our problems will be solved!"

"Sure, church boy," Ray says while laughing and winking at his two associates.

Again I begin to feel a little nervous and ask Ray, "How can we ever repay you?"

It is a rhetorical question, but Ray doesn't let it slip by easily. "Church boy, I'm loaning you this money because that is what we do here. You have ninety days to get it back to me, or we will take whatever collateral we need to fulfill this agreement. Do you understand? This money is yours, so take it and get out of my office. I have other business to attend to, but I'll see you in ninety days!"

As I walk out of the office and the door shuts, I can hear Ray and his two associates laughing. At that moment, I feel as though I've made the biggest mistake ever. I've put my trust in someone whom I really barely know and who has a track record for being on the wrong side of good. Was I a little hasty in my decision? Should I turn around and give him back the money even though I've just told Deacon Harris and Sister

Shirley that I have it? I don't want to look like a failure to the church again, but now I don't know what to do.

Reflective Key Verse

> Lord, how are they increased who trouble me! Many are they who rise up against me. Many are they who say of me, There is no help for him in God. But You, O Lord, are a shield for me; my glory and the One who lifts up of my head. I cried to the Lord with my voice, and He heard me from His Holy hill.

—Psalm 3:1–4

Spiritual Moment

Let's analyze the scenarios that led to the dethroned King David sharing with us through the discourse of this psalm. Although David had sinned with Bathsheba; had murdered her husband, Uriah; and had allowed fear to separate him from trusting in God's protection, we discover here that he had a renewed confidence in God. A source of strength reappeared in his will to continue on.

David, in his attempt to flee from his troubles, took time in a moment of solitude to share with us that the Enemy will launch a campaign of cruel lies against our faith, trying to make it seem as though God has deserted or abandoned our cause. So when his enemies said, "There is no help for him in God," David cried out with all the more assurance, "But thou, O Lord, art a shield for me." In other words, he proclaimed, "Let them say what they will; I am sure thou will never desert me, and I am resolved I will never distrust thee."

In times of trouble and despair, when you need joy and deliverance, keep in your heart, "But You, O Lord, are a shield for me, My glory and the One who lifts up my head" (Psalms 3:2-3). It is God who can and will lift up my head out of my troubles, and restore me to my dignity again, in due time; or, at least, God is able to lift up my head *under* my troubles, so that I shall not droop nor be discouraged, nor shall my spirits fail.

Life Challenge

Under pressure, we may want to throw up our hands. But by doing so, we quickly discover what it means to lose the blessings God has already aligned for us to have. In fact, we can misalign ourselves so much that it seems like God may be distant from us. Have you ever had something happen in your life that caused you to say, "Where is God?"

If, in the worst of times, God's people can lift up their bowed heads with joy, knowing that "all things work together for good to those who love God" (Romans 8:28a), they will know for a fact that it is God that lifts up their heads, that gives them both cause to rejoice and gleeful hearts.

In spite of the opposition or seemingly eminent threat from the Enemy, who seeks to ruin our souls by driving us away from God, we can be encouraged by the ever presence of our God, who owns and protects and will in due time crown His own interest both in the world and in the hearts of His people.

CHAPTER 5

Too Many Excuses

I know your works, that you are neither cold nor hot. I
could wish you were cold or hot. So then, because you
are lukewarm, and neither cold nor hot. I will vomit you
out of My mouth.

—Revelation 3:15–16

Hide and Seek

We'll put a bookmark on Rick, Johnny, Maria, and Pastor Brown for now and pick their stories back up later in the book. Right now I want to talk about what these stories mean for our everyday lives. From time to time, you may hear someone say, "I am the way I am today because of what happened to me in the past." We tend to spend too much time preoccupied with past circumstances still obscuring our future. We all have a past, and if most Christians told the truth, we'd discover shady, dark, and lackluster moments in our lives that we'd sooner forget and place under the heading of *the old me.* Honestly, we *all* have a past.

As Christians, especially men, we tend to masquerade ourselves when we come to church. We hide our hurts and fears with Sunday smiles. We break out in nicely tailored Armani suits, super–shined-up Stacy Adams shoes or Gators, and don't forget the coordinating Italian silk ties and pocket squares. And so this doesn't look one-sided, ladies, you do an even better job by putting on those new Ralph Lauren dresses with matching Gucci purses and Louis Vuitton heels. Once we look the part, now we can commence a game of hide and seek; we are the *great pretenders!* We enter a church and are met by the usher or the greeter, who under his or her own smile asks,

"How are you doing this morning, brother [or sister]?" And of course, from behind the made-up smiles on our faces, we say, "Great! Praise the Lord! Matter of fact, I can't complain about a thing!"

We have become masters of the game of hide and seek, and the sad part about it is most of the time we believe it ourselves. As Christians, we have learned or taught ourselves that it is not okay to show we are dealing with issues in our lives. We try to cover up painful events, broken relationships, and unbearable situations because we think it shows a lack of faith in God.

We must understand that if we didn't have problems, we wouldn't know about faith in God and how He is a problem solver. It doesn't matter how long we've been Christians, we must not deny the fact that our pasts are exactly what help us through this process of change.

"Yes, and all who desire to live godly in Christ Jesus will suffer persecution" (2 Timothy 3:12).

If you've been able to identify with Rick, Johnny, Maria, or Pastor

Brown, then you understand the deep-seated roots of your past and how your past has affected everything about you so far. The strengthening process occurs when we discover our issues and bring them to the forefront of our thoughts; we then are able to remove those painful thorns and eliminate them as constant reminders of days long gone. Are you still hiding behind your past? Our pasts come in various shapes, sizes, and levels of intensity. We often feel they are best kept in the closet or buried. We avoid disturbing them so that they won't be brought into the light or to the surface. The problem is that most of our past trials and tribulations were caused by somebody, and the images of that person, even if we have not even talked to them or know where they are currently, may still dwell in our minds. Let me show you how to move beyond this.

It's Just My Luck

I've discovered over the years as a Christian that the greatest resource and best therapy I could ever receive comes directly to me, no charge, in the Bible. That may be big news to some while others will claim to know that already, but I thought I'd take this opportunity to share it with you anyway. I never take anything for granted. There are countless, timeless answers and solutions given to us by God. All we have to do is learn how to trust in the Lord.

For instance, take a look at this passage of Scripture from the New Testament: "Who delivered us from so great a death, and does deliver us; in whom we trust that He will still deliver us" (2 Corinthians 1:10).

The biggest notion is that if you're having a bad day, which happens sometimes, then either today is not your day to be blessed and highly favored, or you're being tested by God. For some, it may seem that way all the time, but the bottom line is that we can make the best out of every situation we face, whether bad or good. In the Christian life, we should not chalk it up to worldly thinking involving *good* or *bad* luck. We operate in the realm of God's desired will for us, and He allows us to choose our predestined course. Now, based on our own decisions, we enter into situations and conditions that may or may not be favorable in pursuit of God's desired will. Just as written in 2 Corinthians 1:10, we must *trust* that God will deliver us out of the mess of our own doing and set us upon the course He has established already for us.

Life is full of challenges and obstacles. Do you remember the movie *The Wizard of Oz?* Dorothy, a young Kansas farm girl, and her dog, Toto, are whisked away one day as a severe tornado lands their house in the magical Land of Oz. She then embarks on an adventure through Munchkinland along the yellow brick road to the Emerald City, refuge of the great and powerful Wizard of Oz. Along the way, she befriends the Scarecrow, the Tin Man, and the Cowardly Lion, who all decide to join her to personally ask the Wizard for a brain, heart, and courage, respectively. It's a long trip filled with danger and suspense. They have to battle witches, flying monkeys, and their own fears and personal challenges. In spite of the improbability, they refuse to let their personal excuses cause them to fail their mission. They are determined to complete it to the end.

Many of us feel the same way. We're missing certain attributes that will make our lives more fulfilling and successful; however, we lack the perseverance to travel our yellow brick roads to accomplish those goals. Pick yourself up, look forward, and just keep on moving. Your goals are in view if you believe in yourself.

I've discovered that with every excuse that we think of, God has a corresponding answer. Imagine God as the great chess Master with our lives being the chessboard. We make a few moves on our own rather hastily, and before long, we get intimidated by the outcome and probability of losing. But then God steps in and shows us the right move. At that point, He turns it back over to us and says, "Now what are you going to do?"

The Bible teaches us how to be overcomers. God has orchestrated the Bible to be a guide of restoration for those of us who have encountered some ups and downs. It's there for those of us who have failed several times but never quit. The Bible has a lot to teach us about our pain, our problems, and our disappointments, but more than anything, it has a lot to teach us about being living testimonies and joining the I-made-it band. Whatever your situation may be, know this: it is no secret or surprise to God. He is always aware of you and me ... our pasts, presents, and futures.

All of this reminds me of a chapter in my own personal life when God truly demonstrated the power of His will. I was stationed at Camp Pendleton, California, and had entered into the twilight (normally that's the last two years or less) of my United States Marine Corps career of over twenty years. Due to manpower requirements, or so they said, I was given orders to spend a one-year, unaccompanied (without family) tour in Okinawa, Japan. I'll let you in on a little secret: this is one of the places I told myself that I would never go. Well, I'd learned a few years earlier when God had sent me to California that when He wants you to go somewhere, He makes sure you do it. Sounds a little like Jonah from the Bible and his reluctance to go to Nineveh, where God wanted him to go! So I went to Okinawa.

Many things started happening because of my obedience to God, but let's make this story filled with blessings short by getting to the excuse portion. I had developed a relationship with the chaplains based on my previous connections and being a licensed minister myself. I lived in the barracks on Camp Hansen, on the northeastern end of Okinawa and began Bible studies for the Marines. I worked on the base initially, since I didn't have any transportation. Well, one of my long-time friends, who is a fellow Marine from Camp Pendleton, was already stationed there at Camp Hansen. He invited me to come and visit his church service at Kadena Air Force Base where they held a gospel service. Again, God had a plan for me. The chaplain in charge of the service asked me to be in charge of the ministerial staff and become a regular member.

Well, that was only a temporary assignment according to God. I had been asked to conduct a wedding back in California, but before I left, I was asked if I would organize and initiate a Pentecostal gospel service at Camp Kinser, on the far southwestern end of the island. I let the chaplaincy know that I would have to pray about it and let them know when I returned because I did not have transportation and the bus ride every Sunday took me well over an hour from one side to the other one-way.

When I returned with my excuse, God eliminated it immediately. One of my chaplain friends at Camp Hansen, who had received orders to leave the island, knew what I'd been asked to do and handed me the keys to his car so that I could get back and forth, as needed. God is awesome! To make a long story short, God removed the excuse, allowed me to start the gospel service on Camp Kinser and made sure I had room enough to carry some Marines with me each Sunday to church. And to further reward me, God cut my tour of duty short there and returned me back home to California to finish my last year before retiring, using Okinawa, Japan, as a prelude and training ground for the pastorate awaiting me in California. There is no doubt in my mind, that God has a preordained purpose for each of us. It's up to us to live out the plan and realize that God is a Master of removing excuses from our dialogue when it comes to fulfilling His plan.

What Direction Will You Go

Let's take a moment to direct our attention to those of you who, for some reason or another, have actually walked away from Christ.

"From that time many of His disciples went back and walked with Him no more. Then Jesus said to the twelve, 'Do you also want to go away?' But Simon Peter answered Him, 'Lord, to whom shall we go? You have the words of eternal life'" (John 6:66–68).

If we look at the life and ministry of our Lord Jesus Christ while He walked here on this Earth, we notice some hard facts about why some people turned their backs on Him and walked away. Throughout the Gospels, the Scriptures speak of many people following after Jesus out of either belief in Him, curiousity about Him or disdainment for Him. Study the Scriptures for yourself, and you can't help but understand how much of an attraction Jesus was to the people at that time. The great Messiah came down to deliver them and set them free! And then the miracles and wonders He performed before their eyes! Wisdom spawned out of His lips daily during his ministry with the reassurance that the kingdom of heaven was prepared and accessible for all who chose to love and accept God. Jesus' ministry was a great thing to be a part of and drew many, both spectators and new converts.

Can we be imaginative right now? Open up your spiritual eyes and see the gospel stories come alive in your mind. Even if you don't claim to be biblical experts, you can definitely recall the vivid details of Him healing the sick, giving sight to the blind, giving the ability to hear to the deaf, and strengthening limbs for the lame. Can you see Him do it? Can you see Jesus approaching and asking, "Do you want to be made whole again?" Or in other words, "Do you want to be well?"

Jesus is a miracle worker. As we journey through the Gospels, we have a tragic story of Jesus arriving in Bethany apparently too late to help His friend Lazarus, who had been dead and buried for four days. Lazarus' sisters and friends had just come from the funeral, and then Jesus raised Lazarus from the dead. Jesus needs no excuse. How about the time when Jesus showed his disciples that He is the Master Chef? He opened up His spiritual cookbook, took five barley loaves and two fish, and proceeded to feed five thousand. He's a miracle worker. In his three-year earthly ministry, Jesus caused demons to relocate and hushed an angry sea, just to name a few of his miracles. And in the midst of all this, people were still making so many excuses. Miracles, day and night, caused quite a few people to want to be in His crowd to either be a spectator or participant. Now let me throw you a curveball: the Scriptures indicate that following Jesus did not always mean you were a follower of Jesus. Why? Well, I'm glad you asked! There's a difference due to the simple word *why*.

Walk with me figuratively. If I am taking a stroll down the street and I notice you are walking behind me, you are following me, right? But if I go around the block and you continue straight, then you are no longer following me. Now imagine the same scenario, except this time we are headed in the same direction. One of us will end up leading, and the other will end up following from point A to point B. Why? Because we are going to the same place. So the one who is following in this instance is following for the right reason.

Now set your gaze upon Jesus. Many people followed Him then, and multitudes follow Him now, with entirely different reasons. Many follow because they want Him to establish His kingdom on earth and others because they're ready to join Him in heaven.

In the New Testament, the Gospel according to St. Luke tells of a series of incidents occurring with three of Jesus' disciples and their excuses for delaying commitment to following Jesus. Consider this: if our hearts have been adequately prepared to make a difference in others' lives, then a call to duty will always come with a favorable, unhesitating response.

We gain a great deal of insight when we carefully listen to what Jesus expected when He called the disciples to follow Him.

> Now it happened as they journeyed on the road, that someone said to Him, "Lord, I will follow You wherever You go." And Jesus said to him, "Foxes have holes and birds of the air have nests, but the Son of Man has nowhere to lay His head." Then He said to another, "Follow Me." But he said, "Lord, let me first go and bury my father." Jesus said to him, "Let the dead bury their own dead, but you go and preach the kingdom of God." And another also said, "Lord, I will follow You, but let me first go and bid them farewell who are at my house." But Jesus said to him, "No one, having put his hand to the plow, and looking back, is fit for the kingdom of God." (Luke 9:57–62)

Okay, so let's quickly summarize what is going on here. One man wanted to stay in his comfort zone, another wanted to make sure whatever was done was convenient for him, and the last man really wanted to keep his options open and be allowed to make choices based on his timing and schedule. None of those excuses or the ones you have will work for Jesus. He demands total sacrifice and unreserved commitment to follow Him.

Living beyond Our Pasts

As excuses go, even in the Bible great people of God, led by God, play the excuse card instead of taking the time to fully trust in God to handle their situations. When God asked Moses, Noah, Jonah, the children of Israel, and the twelve disciples to do something that they deemed impossible, they all offered God excuses for why He would be better off picking someone else. Just think about it for a moment.

Our pasts have shaped us to be the people we are today. Our pasts are not an indicator of our futures but the reason we've succeeded to a future. Okay, let me say it this way: our trials and tribulations of the past only open the doors to our current and future triumphs and victories. We learn from our mistakes, and if God allows it, we come out of those situations realizing that it could have been worse and that we made it. That's the greatness of God: we get ourselves in trouble, and He is always there to direct us out. My grandma put it this way, "He's a way maker. He's a problem solver. He's a burden sharer and heavy-load bearer." The young folk of today would say, "He's all that and more!" Jesus has a whole life mapped out for His followers. You need to closely follow Him to be on that path. Comforts, convenience, and preserving our life choices always get in the way of following Jesus. What excuse have you chosen to prevent your total love for God? How about now giving these three things up for the Lord? Tell Jesus that you will go anywhere He wants, closely attend to what business He puts before you, and stay consistent to Him all your life, without reservation and with total commitment. What cost are you willing to pay?

Reflective Key Verse

> I know all the things you do, that you are neither hot nor cold. I wish you were one or the other! But since you are like lukewarm water, I will spit you out of my mouth!

—Revelation 3:15–16

Spiritual Moment

As it is written by the apostle John to the church in Laodicea, one of the seven churches he addresses in the Holy Bible, Jesus Christ personally introduced Himself as the amen, the faithful and true witness, and the ruler of God's creation. And speaking to the church in Laodicea, He referred to the people as lukewarm individuals. Jesus said, "I know all the things you do, that you are neither hot nor cold. I wish you were one or the other!" The church thought of itself as rich and in need of nothing from Christ.

It's interesting that Jesus said He would prefer either hot or cold. You would think He would have said, "I would rather you be hot. But if lukewarm is all I can get, it's better than nothing." You would think that lukewarm would be more acceptable to Him because it is somewhat close to hot. But Jesus was saying, "I don't want lukewarm. I don't want halfhearted commitments. I want you to decide. I want you in, or I would rather you were out."

Life Challenge

When I attended John Burroughs Elementary School in Washington, DC, at recess, we were given milk and cookies. Milk is great cold. There's nothing quite like it with cookies. It doesn't matter what your favorite kind is—Oreo, oatmeal, peanut butter—cold milk and cookies are quite a team. Milk is also good hot, on a cold winter day with some cocoa and marshmallows. Mmmm-mmm, good! But drinking lukewarm milk? The thought of it is sickening. It just doesn't cut it.

Here's why! If you're hot, you're in. If you're on fire, if you're walking with God, then you're where God wants you to be. But if you're cold, hopefully you will at least realize you're cold and one day realize your need for Christ and come to Him. But the lukewarm person is in the worst state of all because he or she is self-deceived. The lukewarm person says, "I go to church. I read the Bible sometimes. I kind of believe in God—when it's convenient." That is the worst state of all. What is your spiritual temperature today?

CHAPTER 6

Trouble Doesn't Last Always, or Does It

We are troubled on every side, yet not distressed; we
are perplexed, but not in despair; persecuted, but not
forsaken; cast down, but not destroyed!

—2 Corinthians 4:8–9 KJV

Everywhere I Go, There It Is

Many times in life we become victimized by trouble. Walk up
to anyone, in any part of the world, and ask if he or she has
experienced some type of trouble in life, and most assuredly, that person
will respond yes. Trouble is not exclusive to a certain gender, ethnic
group, political party, geographical setting, economical status, or any
other category you may think of. Isn't it amazing how it seems that
trouble follows some people as closely as their own shadow? No wonder
they can't help but bump into it all the time. Trouble as defined by
Merriam-Webster is "a situation that is difficult or has a lot of problems."

The issue is compounded for those who don't have a personal relationship with Jesus Christ or whose relationship is not as profound and intimate as it should be. Building relationships must entail a certain amount of trust interwoven as a security blanket to help us through life. What happens is that we become emotionally tied to our problems and then become overwhelmed by their effects.

Think about it! When I was growing up, I used to watch a popular television show called *The Flip Wilson Show*. In the show, Flip Wilson often played and dressed as a female character named Geraldine. Geraldine would tell a few jokes, talk about her boyfriend, Killer, and then deliver the famous line "The Devil made me do it!" The audience would erupt into laughter. Later, it became a notable slogan used from time to time, mainly by Christians or people calling themselves Christians but really not acting the part, in order to explain or excuse their reason for doing the wrong thing or messing up. "The Devil made me do it!" What is *it*? *It* is any result of the trouble, circumstance, issue, or failed attempt produced of one's own accord. We tend to blame the Enemy for everything we do wrong or anything out of the scope of God's will, but most of our trouble is spawned within us. Then we turn to external sources to appease our need to remove these obstacles, just to later find out that it didn't help anything but to pamper our feelings. In other words, we turn to friends or professional help only to be given a bunch of opinions or recommendations that fail because they lack the power to change the condition.

Change is often necessary to eliminate conditions that have been a self-destructive force on your road of life. God sometimes wants you to detour off the road that has become too familiar to you. Change is hard but important. People can't promise more than they can produce. God can! Put a bookmark here, and we'll come back to this thought that will bless your socks off!

Making the Best out of a Bad Situation

I remember at my church, Ebenezer Baptist Church in Occoquan, Virginia, the Robert "Pop" Middleton Male Chorus sang many gospel greats, including an old song titled "Trouble Don't Last Always" written by Reverend Timothy Wright. As we go through life and grow older, we discover more than we'd care to learn, know, and experience about trouble. The song's repeated words "Trouble don't last always" have become a part of my conscious awareness of God's sustaining power.

The lesson I've learned based on my relationship with Christ is that He is greater than any issue, trouble, or obstacle I may face in life. Though problems may be present, they are not permanent. Confinement, bad reports, pink slips, and family losses should not stop you from proceeding with God's direction. Stand on your Enemy's head, and continue to work because it is an outgoing process. The work of the Lord should go forward, with power! We should make every effort to see the kingdom of God succeed.

In the Apostle Paul's life, the days of open doors were gone. Paul was in prison, and all the doors were barred, locked, closed, and no longer accessible. He was chained up and held in bondage. Paul wanted to help others but found himself unavailable because of his own plight. How did Paul deal with his situation? Faith helped Paul and can help us too. Faith lifts up people's eyes, and even in prison, in bondage, in a bad situation, there is opportunity. What shall the verdict be? Believe in God. The reason why trouble doesn't last always is because of the theological purpose injected into the circumstance. God allows trouble to come our way for a season as a test of our faith in Him. God gives us faith as a reminder of His power to deliver us from any circumstance or problem that weighs us down like an anchor. The task of faith is to overcome. Faith does not explain itself. Sometimes you will not know why you are going through what you are going through. Certain factors that occur in our lives cannot always be addressed with an easy explanation, but faith allows us to make the best of our bad situations. Faith allows us to be overcomers to the mysteries that life presents before us through the blood of Jesus Christ.

Make the most of your troubles, because when you come out, you will come out with a testimony, a praise report, and a reassurance that God can and will… time after time. Faithfulness challenges us and allows us to explore what God has already promised.

Look at the story of Joseph, son of Jacob, in the book of Genesis. Circumstances placed Joseph in a pit by the hands of his very own brothers!

> Now when they saw him afar off, even before he came near them, they conspired against him to kill him. Then they said to one another, Look, this dreamer is coming! Come therefore, let us now kill him and cast him into some pit; and we shall say, some wild beast has devoured him. We shall see what will become of his dreams! But Reuben heard it, and he delivered him out of their hands, and said, Let us not kill him. And Reuben said to them, Shed no blood, but cast him into this pit which is in the wilderness, and do not lay a hand on him—that he might deliver him out of their hands, and bring him back to his father. So it came to pass, when Joseph had come to his brothers, that they stripped Joseph of his tunic, the tunic of many colors that was on him. Then they took him and cast him into a pit. And the pit was empty; there was no water in it. (Genesis 37:18–24)

See what can happen with just a little sibling hatred? Joseph became the target of a great deal of trouble; however, his situation could have been worse. He could have been killed and buried in the pit. He could have been eaten by wild, hungry beasts passing by. Instead, his brothers sold him into slavery to the Ishmaelites for twenty shekels of silver. Despite his circumstances, Joseph was taken to Egypt and rose to the honorable position of governor. This was truly a great pit-to-palace success story. What was meant for evil by his brothers God turned around for Joseph's good. "But as for you, you meant evil against me; but God meant it for good, in order to bring it about as it is this day, to save many people alive" (Genesis 50:20).

Life is a journey, and every one of us is on it. We may surmise that our journeys are different, but if you truly think about it and ascertain some factual evidence, we may conclude that our journeys are the same. Everything Joseph experienced, you will experience too! You begin your journey with the favor of God and a dream. The beauty of the dream is shattered by the reality of the pit. Just when you think things can't get worse, they do. A crisis is required to test your character. You find out quickly who you really are in God when you are in the pit. The pit is not your destiny. The pit is temporary until God unveils your destiny. Your destiny is the palace.

The greatest test of faith is when life shows its worst side; if it never gets bad, who needs faith? But when you get down and out and trouble surrounds you, when it looks like you are going down for the last count, that's when Jesus steps in. It seems that the worse the problem, the better the testimony. Victory comes by passing the tests of life that challenge our resolve and determine who we really are.

Don't you know that the Devil (Satan, Lucifer, the tempter, Beelzebub, Diablo, or whatever you call him) hates men and women of faith and desires to bring down your house of faith? You go through life, and it all amounts to how you handle your problems. In other words, two people may have the same problem, and one will give up while the other will sing for joy anyhow. We can make a bad situation worse by not leaning on our faith. Don't let the Devil think he has you on the run; instead stand boldly on Jesus! We are shaped by our lives' circumstances. God builds us up through our hard days, our difficult times, our shipwrecks, our poverty, and our losses. We can appreciate that it was those hard days that allow us to shout for joy now: "Look where He's brought us from." Victory can be yours!

This bad situation is about to bring you to your greatest moment. Things that have happened to me could have caused me to walk around with my head bowed down, saying, "Lord, You called me, and if I'm not meant to be where I am, place me where You want me to be. I will rejoice anyhow!"

If it's good, rejoice, and if it's bad, still rejoice! The Bible says, "And we know that all things work together for good to those who love God," (Romans 8:28a). God is getting ready to turn you around, bring you through, break you out, *and* lift you up. Can I encourage you? Every bad thing that has happened to you, stop crying, stop looking defeated, and do yourself a favor and say, "I will lift up mine eyes to the hills- From whence comes my help? My help *comes* from the Lord, Who made heaven and earth." (Psalm 121)

Joy in the Midst of Your Trouble

No biblical discussion or narrative about living a joyous life and overcoming obstacles would ever be complete without mentioning the apostle Paul. Paul seems almost larger than life because his joy knew no bounds. As you read through his letters, it seems that the greater the trial he faced, the greater his joy. His life is a living illustration of severe affliction intermingled with supreme joy. Paul's missionary journeys placed him in many perilous conditions, including being put in chains as a prisoner in a Roman jail after being shipwrecked and barely surviving.

Chapters 21–28 of the book of Acts explain how Paul ended up in Rome. It began with his return to Jerusalem after his third missionary journey. To affirm he was still living in obedience to the law, he went to the temple to participate in a ceremony. There, after being accused of teaching against the law and violating the temple, he was attacked by a mob. He might have been killed had he not been rescued by Roman soldiers. They kept him in custody to protect him. He later spent two years as a prisoner in Caesarea and then another two years under house arrest back in Rome. He was not put in a prison with other criminals because he had not committed any crime against Roman law. The Roman authorities probably realized there was no real criminal charge against Paul, yet because they could not release him before his case was adjudicated, they allowed him to be a private prisoner in his own quarters.

Paul's joy was unrelated to his circumstances. If his joy had been tied to pleasures on earth, possessions, freedom, prestige, outward success, or a good reputation, he wouldn't have had any joy. Paul's joy was centered on his ministry. In his ministry, he discovered joy in spite of trouble, haters, threats, and the possibility of death.

A Christian's spiritual maturity can be measured by what it takes to steal his or her joy. Joy is part of the fruit of a Spirit-controlled life. "But the fruit of the Spirit is love, joy, peace, longsuffering, kindness, goodness, faithfulness, gentleness, self-control" (Galatians 5:22–23a).

In all circumstances, the Spirit of God produces joy, so there ought not to be any time when we're not rejoicing in some way. "Rejoice in the

Lord always. Again I will say, rejoice!" (Philippians 4:4).

To live Christian lives, we should not allow circumstances to displace our feeling of joy with depression, bitterness, or negativity. The one thing that will rob us of our joy is sin. It is then that we cry out like the psalmist, "Restore to me the joy of Your salvation, And uphold me by Your generous Spirit" (Psalm 51:12). Nothing short of sin should steal our joy. But change, confusion, trials, tribulations, spiritual and physical attacks, unmet desires, conflict, and strained relationships can throw us off balance and rob us of our joy if we are not watchful and prayerful.

Jesus Christ actually warned us about trouble in John 16:33: "These things I have spoken to you, that in Me you may have peace. In the world you will have tribulation; but be of good cheer, I have overcome the world." Before I joined the Marine Corps, I came across a thought-provoking recruiting poster that spoke of our lives and what Jesus is referring to in John 16:33. The classic poster was of a short Marine drill instructor wearing his campaign cover (affectionately called the Smokey Bear hat) and glaring sternly upward into the eyes of a new recruit. On the poster, the caption read, "We Don't Promise You a Rose Garden."

Before you drift into a pity party and think, *What is the point anyhow?* Let me remind you of a statement from the apostle James that I keep close to my heart: "Consider it pure joy, my brothers and sisters, whenever you face trials of many kinds, because you know that the testing of your faith produces perseverance" (James 1:2–3 NIV)

God has a purpose for us that He predestined before we actually appeared on the scene. That is our reassurance as we go through the stuff in life that causes us to suffer; Jesus Christ offers blessed assurance as a reason for our joy. To maintain our joy, we must adopt God's perspective regarding our trials. When we allow God's will and Spirit to be in every aspect of our lives and we yield to Him, our difficulties will not overwhelm us.

God has provided thorns to keep us mindful of His strength and Power, but the beauty comes with our holding on to the rose of Sharon ... our Jesus! Let's pause right here and just be thankful that our rough times haven't destroy us but instead built us up so that we can be shown by God to be victorious overcomers. I'm so glad that I've learned how to endure the test and count it all as joy!

I've Arrived at Nevertheless

Just as Jesus suffered in His ministry and many of the early Christians suffered, still today Christians are suffering. We will always experience suffering, of some type, along this walk we've chosen. After all, when we decide to follow Jesus Christ, He desires us to be faithful to the end. Let's go back to the apostle Paul!

Paul was faithful in spite of his trials and tribulations. Paul was faithful to the end because of his choice to follow Jesus Christ. Jesus wants us to be like His faithful servant Paul. Paul didn't give up. Trouble surrounded him many times, but he knew at all times, that God would see him through his troubles. And he also remembered that our troubles don't last always.

Imagine the scene at the garden of Gethsemane at the foot of the Mount of Olives just outside of Jerusalem. The Passover supper has been eaten. Jesus has concluded His Upper Room Discourse, as recorded in John's gospel. Jesus and the disciples leave the upper room and cross over the Kidron to the Mount of Olives and directly to the garden of Gethsemane. The cross now looms large on the horizon.

Then Jesus came with them to a place called Gethsemane, and said to the disciples, "Sit here while I go and pray over there." And He took with Him Peter and the two sons of Zebedee, and He began to be sorrowful and deeply distressed. Then He said to them, "My soul is exceedingly sorrowful, even to death. Stay here and watch with Me." He went a little farther and fell on His face, and prayed, saying, "O My Father, if it is possible, let this cup pass from Me; nevertheless, not as I will, but as You will." Then He came to the disciples and found them sleeping, and said to Peter, "What! Could you not watch with Me one hour? Watch and pray, lest you enter into temptation. The spirit indeed is willing, but the flesh is weak." Again, a second time, He went away and prayed, saying, "O My Father, if this cup cannot pass away from Me unless I drink it, Your will be done." And He came and found them asleep again, for their eyes were heavy. So He left them, went away again, and prayed the third time, saying the same words. Then He came to His disciples and said to them, "Are you still sleeping and resting? Behold, the hour is at hand, and the Son of Man is being betrayed into the hands of sinners. Rise, let us be going. See, My betrayer is at hand." (Matthew 26:36–46)

Judas and the arresting party arrive and arrest Jesus. He is tried and then crucified on the cross with all the accompaniment of pain, torment, humiliation, and shame. The cross was not only near in time but was also heavy on the mind of our Savior while here in the garden.

Let me pause for a moment to underscore this important point: Jesus Christ had to die on the cross so that we (mankind) could have life eternally. Theologically, there was no other way for us to receive salvation from our sins but through the innocent, sacrificial, and substitutionary suffering and death of our Lord and Savior, Jesus Christ. He went to the cross at Calvary not for Himself but for you and me.

In the garden, Jesus' prayer and cries to the Father were for us. It was there where Jesus told God, the Father, *nevertheless*. Say it with Me. *Nevertheless*. Just like our Savior, Jesus Christ, I've arrived at this word— n*evertheless*. If you don't remember anything else, remember this simple word that will help you when you face obstacles, when life throws you curveballs, when it looks like you're heading toward a dead end.

Each test has a purpose, and each test will make you wiser and stronger. Everything that you and I go through is working out for our good. Yes, it hurts. I know you want to give up, but you can't. Stay with Jesus! "I will lift up my eyes to the hills-from whence comes my help?" (Psalm 121:1). Don't you know that "Trouble don't last always." Oh my, can't you feel it? It's your time to be blessed because I know for a fact and have been convinced that "Trouble don't last always."

Reflective Key Verse

> We are troubled on every side, yet not distressed; we are perplexed, but not in despair; persecuted, but not forsaken; cast down, but not destroyed!
>
> —2 Corinthians 4:8–9 KJV

Spiritual Moment

We may be afflicted, perplexed, persecuted, and struck down in the cause for Christ. However, if we, in the time of our need, simply humble ourselves before the mighty hand of God and avail ourselves of the surpassing greatness of His power, though afflicted, we will not be crushed; though perplexed, we will not be despaired; though persecuted, we will not be forsaken; though knocked down, we will not be destroyed. This truth will cause us to embrace whatever rejection and suffering we may experience in the cause for Christ and seek to live lives pleasing to Him as an opportunity for the power of God to be put on display.

Therefore, may God give us the grace to understand that when our weakness is exposed by the difficulties of living for Christ, it is then that we have an opportunity for the awesomeness of God's power to shine forth brightly!

Life Challenge

> Jesus answered and said unto them, Verily I say unto you, If ye have faith, and doubt not, ye shall not only do this which is done to the fig tree, but also if ye shall say unto this mountain, Be thou removed, and be thou cast into the sea; it shall be done. And all things, whatsoever ye shall ask in prayer, believing, ye shall receive.
>
> —Matthew 21:21–22 KJV

Many of us have been around the Word of God long enough to know that there is power in the spoken word. "We can have what we say" (Mark 11:23) only when it is based upon God's ultimate will. Jesus is talking about finding a scriptural promise for something and speaking it forth with the words of our mouths. In Matthew 21:21 where Jesus referred to speaking to a mountain, He was referring to mountains of human obstacles or problems.

We can take the Word of God and stand up to any obstacle that confronts us, commanding the obstacle to be removed, and it must obey. That's good news to all of us who believe and have faith to trust. If your obstacle is sickness, you can take one or more of any of the healing promises of the Bible and move that mountain of sickness by the words of your mouth. If your obstacle is financial, emotional, moral, social, and so on, God has already spoken in agreement to do something about your obstacle. Now it's up to us to speak the promise of God (or the solution He has already prescribed in His Word) over the obstacle (or the problem).

We ought to not think of it as being peculiar when a fiery trial comes upon us. It isn't strange. Many have suffered. Many have struggled. Many have been challenged by disappointment. Many have felt daily pressures trying to destroy their confidence in life. Many have faced their fiery furnace like the three Hebrew boys. Many have had their lives changed, but for the better. Remember Peter, Jesus' right-hand man? Oh, how suffering changed Peter. Rejoice! Push your way through the storm. Rejoice! Push your way through your struggles. Rejoice! Push your way through your valleys. Rejoice! Push your way up the rough side of the mountain. Rejoice! Push your way when it seems like all hope is gone. Rejoice! Push your way through alcoholism, through drug addiction, through abuse, and rejoice! I say rejoice because "Trouble don't last always."

Yes, I know it's hard, but you have to know that Jesus is with you and guiding you through your personal storms. Think of how bad it would be if Jesus wasn't with you in the midst of the storm holding back the winds and the waves of the sea. Stop looking at the situations and the circumstances of this life, and focus on glory. Focus on the Master of the seas. Focus on the Creator of everything. Focus on the Alpha and the Omega, the beginning and the end. Focus on Him!

If your head is bowed down at this moment and you feel like you just can't make it, take the advice found in Psalm 24: 7–10:

Lift up your heads, O you gates! And be lifted up, you everlasting doors! And the King of glory shall come in. Who is this King of glory? The LORD strong and mighty. The LORD mighty in battle. Lift up your heads, O you gates! Lift up, you everlasting doors! And the King of glory shall come in. Who is this King of glory? The LORD of hosts, He is the King of glory.

You know that at the end of the storm is *your bright side*. Yes, there is a lily of the valley, and it is as bright as the morning star. There is a rose of Sharon springing up in the midst of your desert, and your breakthrough is *here*. Your deliverance is *here*.

Oh my, can't you feel it? It's your time to be blessed, because "Trouble don't last always."

CHAPTER 7

Meeting at the Crossroads

Blessed is the man who endures temptation: for when he
has been approved, he will receive the crown of life which
the Lord has promised to those who love Him.

—James 1:12

People Reaching People

The many episodes, phases, junctures, chapters, or however you
define your life are truly amazing. These are the moments in time
from birth to death, from cradle to grave, that makes us who we are and
who we are to become as we forever hold on to the lingering memories
of who we once were. Every one of us has a story to be told. But the
simple fact is that when you get to the end of the story, what does it say
about that person's life? Will the end of your story be some theatrical and
entertaining rewrite with a slow-moving epic climb to the top, followed
by thunderous applause? Or will it be a constant passing of time until

you've concluded and have nothing left behind to show or share with anyone? It's up to us!

Rick's Story Recap

A Soldier's Story

So journey back with me to a four-cornered room and Rick Bosley.

Who would have ever thought *that I would end up like this ... a real nowhere man? No reason to live any longer. Just look at me: Richard "Rick" Bosley. A highly decorated Vietnam War veteran and hero. America's finest and one of the few who made it out of my little country town in the hills of Pennsylvania. Look at me. I've become a broken shell of a man.*

Depressive thoughts and feelings of uselessness overwhelmed me. Looking up at a paint-chipped ceiling, I shouted, "Who can I protect now when I can't even help myself?"

I sat there, day in and day out, staring at the walls of my empty room...desolate, lifeless, and lonely. It was a room filled with so many memories that utterly haunted me, a room that had been like a prison to me, a man who had done so much to make our nation free and secure for all. The room had seemed so large when I was growing up, but now it seemed hardly large enough for me to move around. It seemed to be closing in on me by the minute.

Why had life dished me such a rotten egg? Why me? Why, after all I had done and tried to do for my country? I peered endlessly at the drab four corners and asked myself, "Why was I dealt such an awful hand?"

Kenny Rogers wrote a song about a gambler, and as I sat there, I thought about the words to that song. *Do you suppose that was me, and now I'm awakening from my dream world to face reality?* I had gambled

108

away the good fortunes of my life to come to this point of decision with tiny voices in my head telling me to "hold 'em or fold 'em."

It's hard when you decide on a plan for your life and begin executing the plan, and then the course you've set is altered. Thoughts of depression and failure drop into Rick's head like a bunch of army paratroopers. He makes up his mind to leave his small country town in Pennsylvania after graduating from high school and then pursue a career in the army. Well, Rick did not anticipate that his army career would be so short-lived and that he'd wind up back home in that same town he'd worked so hard to leave. Visiting is one thing—to see how the folks and old friends are doing—but Rick has been medically discharged from the army and sent back home for good.

They kept me in that VA hospital for about two years trying to rehab me, but I just lay in bed thinking, *What's the use? Doc, I have no legs! I will never walk again!*

The doctors kept telling me that they could train me how to walk again on prosthetic legs, but where was the money going to come from to pay for them? I lay there and for days saw many guys that looked just like me—missing something and struggling through life with no hope left in their eyes. All around me lay remnants of the tragedies of war. Yes, people called me a *hero*, but I struggled with that label since I didn't make the kind of big impact in the war that I had been trained to do. I imagined myself killing a bunch of them VCs and blowing up more enemy stuff than anybody ever did. I wanted my skills to make a difference, not end this way.

Well, I guess eventually they decide they need my bed for someone else. I wake up early one morning, thinking that it will be routine as usual. Instead they bring me discharge papers. Discharge papers? The orderlies don't take long packing up my trash and getting me ready for my bon voyage out of this place. Just the day before, the doctor came into my room with this big pep talk, saying that if I work hard at it, I will be able to walk again. Easy for the doc to say—he has both his legs and has probably not seen a day of combat in his life. Now I just smirk to myself as I roll out the front door of the hospital. Being fully uniformed, I pause to salute the flag in the center court and then allow the orderlies to help me get on the bus.

I guess I'll be home soon, I think as the doors of the bus close. We start the trip down the road.

Guess Who's Coming to Dinner

It seems almost like I just left. You see, in a small town like mine, nothing really changes. Everything appears to be the same. The bus pulls up, and a couple of the guys help me off and back into my chair. I think, where *is the welcome-home parade?* As minutes roll by, I wonder if I'll have to roll myself all the way home. I sent Ma a telegram to let her know I was coming home. An hour passes, and finally my brother Tommy shows up in Pa's old pickup truck. Perfect! He can throw me and my chair in the back of the truck. I can see by Tommy's expression that he's really not sure what to do. He's happy to see me but at a loss for words. I suppose there will be many in town who'll have that same look when they see me.

"Big Brother, how are you? I mean, sorry for being late! Ma forgot to mention I needed to be here at three to pick you up. But I'll have you home in a jiffy. Bet you miss some of Ma's vittles," Tommy says as he perks up a little and loads me into the truck.

"Tommy, you look good, and I can't wait to get out of this uniform and stuff some of Ma's home cookin' in my gut. Let's get rolling!" I say, laughing to break the ice.

On the way home, Tommy fills me in on everything. My sisters, Loretta and Louise, are both married and living in Hanover County with their husbands and kids. My brother Ben took a job driving trucks in Georgia, and Tommy decided to stay around the farm to help out Ma since Pa hardly ever leaves the house anymore.

"Pa just sits around with his bottle in hand yelling at the dog. I reckon he just mad at the world," Tommy says. He also mentions that Old Man Jackson passed away last winter from pneumonia. His wife is still running the store.

It's hard when you look around and find little appreciation in life anymore. Most of the guys I knew either in school or working in the coal mines have moved away, barely surviving themselves, or have died. The mining business has been hard on many families, not just mine. Many families lost loved ones either from a mining accident or the after-effects of working in the mines. And once they started closing the mines down, many families just packed up and left town. The little town wasn't much before, and now it's an even smaller town with even less going on.

We finally arrive home. Pa's on the front porch sitting in his chair, yelling at the dog, just like Tommy said. I can smell the flavors of home pouring out of the screen door. Ma runs out to see me, but as Tommy pulls my chair down and lowers me into it, I can see the shock on my parents' faces.

"Ma and Pa, your soldier is home!" I say gleefully.

Ma just smiles. Pa takes a quick glance, audibly says, "Yep!" and then takes a chug from his liquor bottle.

I guess the parade is tomorrow. Welcome home, hero! I think. Then I ask, "Ma, what's for supper? There's nothing like home sweet home!"

God Says, "Hold 'Em"

Every morning, I wake up, throw on some clothes, pull myself into my wheelchair, and roll myself into the kitchen and then onto the front porch. A couple of hours later, Pa makes his way out as well, and we both just sit there, gazing over the farm. Not much left of it either—no crops, just a small vegetable garden Ma planted years ago and maintains for when times get rough. I really didn't get to spend much time with Tommy. After the day he picked me up from the bus stop and brought me home, he's been off and gone…I guess some folk don't know how to be around someone like me! I spend a lot of time daydreaming about when I was a kid running around the yard chasing chickens and stuff like that.

I had a therapist coming by, but that stopped last month … I guess they figured out that I didn't want them around me so they didn't need to keep coming by here trying to make me walk. As long as the VA keeps sending me my check every month, I can make it the best I know how without all the pain and frustration. Besides, Ma doesn't mind me being here. I keep her and Pa company, even though neither Pa nor I can do much around the house to help. Some days, Pa yells at me instead of the dog. I bet the dog thinks that is great, me taking him off the hook. I wonder if I will become as angry toward life as Pa. It's hard when you start feeling sorry for yourself. Nobody comes to visit me, and there's no way for me to go anywhere. I don't have any friends. I just sit in my room, staring at the walls and wishing the bomb had finished me off, because then I'd really be a hero—not this half of a man.

One day, as I contemplate my next move, with thoughts of suicide on my mind, I hear a series of rather rhythmic knocks on the screen door. "I hope that therapist isn't back again to pester me about walking," I say to myself. "Ma, who's that knocking at the door? I don't feel like talking to anyone today," I yell in an angry tone.

"Now, that's no way to greet your old buddy!" Staff Sergeant Denny O'Reilly boldly says with that country twang ringing in his voice as he walks into the room.

"My stars! Denny, where did you come from? How did you find me?" I ask, still with that bewildered look on my face.

"I heard you got yourself up and injured over there in 'Nam, and by the time I was able to look you up, they had released you from the hospital. They told me they sent you back home, and you'd told me about this place, so here I am."

"I'm so happy to see you! I heard you were doing pretty good at that EOD instructor school. You're a big-time staff sergeant now! What else are you doing now?" I ask, grinning from ear to ear.

We reminisce about our army days and times together. Then the subject switches back to Vietnam and what happened on that day when I lost my legs. I am so engulfed with my own anger issues and feelings of guilt for surviving the blast, only to become a burden to my family, that I fail to initially notice that Denny is walking around with a pronounced limp. It finally dawns on me as Denny walks over to grab a glass of lemonade from the counter.

"Denny, what happened to you?" I ask, curious.

"A couple of years ago, I had an accident during a training exercise, and wouldn't you know it, I didn't get out of the blasting zone of one of my own rigged bombs. The fragments severed my left leg at the knee. So

113

the army put this wooden leg on me and taught me how to walk again. They even offered me a desk job, but I decided to take the money and run," Denny says.

The next couple of hours we talk about how Denny was able to adjust to life after the injury and how he is coping. In fact, so many questions pour out of me that a sense of remorse starts to replace the anger inside of me.

Denny recalls the moment of his accident and how he just wanted to take his own life to finish the job. He says, "But a voice inside of me kept telling me, 'I have a plan for your life if you trust Me.' I never really went to church or talked to God, but I knew it was Him talking to me. God gave me strength to continue and start my life over again. And guess what else! I'm getting married in a few weeks, and I want you to be my best man."

"I'm so happy for you!" I say. "But my pa always taught us boys that only women prayed and talked to God and that men like us were strong enough to handle anything without Him."

Evidently having overheard the conversation from his bedroom window, my pa rolls out on the front porch and says with tears rolling down his face, "Son, I was wrong and have asked God to forgive me for not recognizing it was Him who saved my life. The day that mine caved in on top of me and the others, everyone else was buried under the rubble. A support beam lying across my chest kept my upper body from getting crushed also. People said that it was a miracle, and over the years, they kept saying it until it finally hit me that it was God! God saved me! God can turn your life around too if you just believe in Him. I pray you let Him and let go of that bitterness! I know I'm one to talk, but something changed inside of me this morning when I woke up. If

He can change me and your friend here, He can do the same for you!"

All three of us simultaneously look up to the sky with tears streaming down our faces and a new radiance shining upon us. All at once, the anger and frustration melt away from me. The change in my pa and his prayer almost immediately lift the burden of how I saw himself as half a man and not fit to live, replacing it with a feeling that I am a man with something worth living for, because of God!

Pa leans toward me and says, "Son, ask Jesus to come into your life right now, and He will renew your life. Jesus has a plan for you and me!"

"Pa, I believe you're right! God, forgive me too!" I say while smiling and feeling a sense of relief.

The next day, Tommy drives me, Pa, and Denny to the bus depot in town.

"I'll send you that wedding invitation when I get back, but hurry yourself over to the VA hospital and tell them they owe you a couple of legs. I want you standing tall next to me, soldier," Denny says and then tucks some chewing tobacco in his mouth.

"Count on it!" I say as Pa and I wave good-bye. We then start on down the road in the truck. On the way home, we decide to stop at the Jackson store to pick up some groceries for Ma.

"Hello, Mrs. Jackson, how are you? We need to pick up a few things to take home," says Pa.

As I approach the counter, Mrs. Jackson says, "Rick, are you very busy these days? I could really use your help running the cash register here at the store. My husband really liked you, and I know you would be a big help for me."

Before I can utter a word, Pa says, "I can get some fellas to haul some lumber over from my barn, and we can build a ramp, right here behind the counter for Rick's chair. We can get it done in about a day, if we really work hard at it. We can grab Tommy's friend Hank and some tools and be back in an hour. What do you say, Son?"

"That will be perfect! Rick, will you accept my offer?" asks Mrs. Jackson with a soft smile on her face.

"Sure thing, Mrs. Jackson! I'll gladly come to work for you, if you think I can do the job."

"My husband believed in you, and I do too! Thank God for you coming back home and stopping by the store. I've been so overwhelmed and was thinking about just closing down the store, but now I won't have to," Mrs. Jackson joyfully says.

We load back up into the truck, and Tommy drives us back home to pick up the lumber. Pa and I continue to talk and laugh together, in a way that we've never done before.

"Pa, it's amazing! A couple of days ago I wanted to cuss God and die. But now, I feel that God has given me a new chance. I have a lot to live for now. And, Pa, don't make that ramp and riser permanent. I need to schedule my appointment with the VA hospital to get those new legs, remember! I have some chicken chasing to do. I'll race ya!"

They both laughed and rejoiced together as they drove home. It's amazing how the love of God can change a person's whole outlook on life. It's like a rebirth. I'm reminded of the Bible story about the Prodigal Son. Rick was lost to the world, but now he's home—Father and son back together again. Let's celebrate a new lease on life!

Johnny's Story Recap

A Gangster's Story

So here I am cornered by the cops. Somebody must have snitched about the shooting, and the worst part about it all is that I can still smell the gunpowder all over my hands. I'm not sure if it is pure adrenaline—maybe a sense of invincibility or some fear of the inevitable, I don't know—but now the same thought keeps running through my mind: *What should I do?* This will be my third strike if I turn myself in, and if I'm convicted of just the murder charges, not to mention the other crimes on my rap sheet, I'm done. The judge will lock me away for good because now I have murder added to my already-large resume, and the weapon is still in my hand. I've seen the *Godfather, Scarface, Dillinger,* and *Goodfellas,* you know the movies. Maybe if I shoot it out, I can get away and escape to Canada or Mexico. Yes, I could sip fancy drinks on the beach in Jamaica with my ladies. I could actually live pretty good. Or I could wind up dead on a cold slab in the morgue. *What should I do?*

Too many voices in my head are pulling me to both extremes, but what will I gain going out like this?

I hadn't imagined I, Johnny "Black Jack" Taylor, of all people, would now be facing a lifetime behind bars. It seems like a never-ending stream of sirens come to a screeching halt all around the building.

Again, the cops give me one more opportunity. "Come out with your hands up, or we're coming in!"

At that moment, I swear I hear my mom's and pops's voices saying, "It's going to be all right, Son! Just come out and give yourself up. Everything will work out."

I'm not really sure if the voices are real or just wishful thinking, but just that quickly, I drop my gun on the floor, raise my hands above my head, and slowly walk out the door into the tension-filled night. As I step out, I can see police crouched everywhere beside their cars, guns pulled and aimed directly at me. There must be about a hundred or more, just to bring me down. I guess they heard about me, "Black Jack" Taylor.

Again, the familiar shout comes from one of the cops in front of me, while several others rush toward me. "You're under arrest; keep your hands up!" You would have thought I shot someone famous as they grab me, throw me on the ground, slap the cuffs on me while reading me my rights, and then cram me into the cop car.

I've been arrested many times, sat in the back of a squad car many times, and been locked up many times, but something inside of me is creeping in. I remember the first time I was arrested for waving that replica gun around on Crenshaw Boulevard at those three punks. I felt like a real man and boasted about my first time in the joint! Okay, it was the county juvie hall, but to a lot of kids, that would have been a wake-up call. Not for me! For me, it was my big step into manhood. Every time after that first time, it was like a notch in my gangster cane. You know what I'm saying? To a gangster, it was like a badge of honor, a rite of passage into the big league of gangsters.

This time, unlike any other time, I felt all alone and that this was it for me! Oh yes, I'd be in the big house all right—penitentiary! Not the huge, fancy white mansion with cameras and guards all around like in *Scarface*. No sitting by my own Olympic-size pool sipping mai tais or some other exotic drink with pretty little paper umbrellas. No harem of fine ladies to wait on my every desire. No fleet of luxury rides... no private jet... no fast loot. All I have to look forward to now is... *time!* This time, fear of the unknown has crept inside me, and it really doesn't feel good at all.

What about Tomorrow?

Even though, in my own mind, I had a great reason for avenging the death of my friend Kenny, others do not think the same way. I am being held in jail without bail and being tried for two counts of murder. As a matter of fact, they've brought up so much against me that my attorney wants me to accept a plea bargain.

I refuse and tell my attorney with a hint of anger, "We were just minding our own business, and then those thugs came in, robbed the 7-Eleven, and shot Kenny. He died because I asked him to go with me to pick up a pack of smokes for my pops. Of course, justice needed to be done, and the cops couldn't find the hoods that did it and didn't seem to be trying very hard. Another black teenage male shot down in his prime. Here we go again! News flash! Black-on-black crime, who cares? Well, I cared, and I found them. Yeah, that's right! As luck would have it, they owed a debt, and I collected. I found them, and I evened the score, making things right for Kenny!"

My attorney shakes his head and says, "But there are witnesses who saw what you did and how you did it, and one of your own men will be testifying against you! He claims you did all the shooting yourself. You were arrested with the murder weapon in your possession. And you admit you did it as a form of vengeance as retribution for your friend's killing. Johnny, that's admirable, but if you don't accept the plea bargain, you're surely going to get the chair!"

"Okay, okay! What choice do I have anyway? I did the crime and don't feel bad at all. They got what they deserved, and Kenny is good now. He can rest easy knowing that I didn't let his killers go unpunished for what they did. I'm sorry for a lot of things I've done but not for this. I'll take the plea bargain and do the time behind bars instead of being fried!" I say reluctantly.

So I take the plea deal. The jury doesn't take long at all rendering a verdict of guilty on the lesser charges of manslaughter, since I did not plan to kill anyone. The judge sees it differently since I admitted to the crime and said my plan was to make them pay for what they had done to my friend. He says that I have a long criminal record and a history of recurring violence. Also, my past and current associations with other known criminal elements make me a "menace to society." The judge wastes no time changing the verdict to second-degree murder and sentencing me to twenty-five to life in prison. Well, he's right, and I accept my punishment. The way I was going, this pattern of mine would have only gotten worse on my climb upward as a *hood*. It was always meant to be since I was a kid. I've always said that I'm a product of the streets where I came from. Statistically, I guess I'm right. At least I didn't get the death penalty.

Before I'm sent to prison, I sit in county jail pondering my future. *While I wait, I think, I'm never going to be free again, and I'm never again going to see most of the people I know. All I have to look forward to is wasting the rest of my life in a prison cell. Why not just end all the pain and suffering now?*

Mom and Pops come to visit me nearly every day. Their visits give me renewed hope in living, even though it's behind bars. I continue to justify my reason for the shooting, which only makes Mom sadder. She has a difficult time believing that I committed murder and became this coldhearted criminal that the judge portrayed me as in court. Even though I know he was right about me, I still want Mom to see me as her little boy. On one of their visits, she tells me that she blames it all on Pops for not being there to teach me. She gets a little loud, and before you know it, the guard looks pretty irritated and is ready to end my visitation time early by escorting both of them out. Pops convinces him that everything is all right and that they won't get loud again. He gives Mom a look as he says this.

"Mom, Pops had nothing to do with me turning out to be what I am! A man learns how to protect what is his, and all I've been doing is getting and protecting," I say to take some of the pressure off of Pops for the moment. "Everything will be all right! I did the crime, so I deserve to be here, and I have to live with it. I had to do it, and I hope you understand." Tears are running down my face.

Mom, still in tears, nods her head in agreement and reaches over to grab Pops's hand. Pops consoles her and says that they have to leave now but will be back in a day or so. Visitations are always good when you're locked up because they break the solemnness of being held behind bars—just knowing that somebody cares enough about you in spite of the crime you committed. Mom and Pops coming together is special for me. I know they blame themselves for the way I turned out, but it was really inside me. I grew up in the hood, and the hood is always in me! I was fooling myself and almost believed that living with Pops, getting good grades, going to college, and having nice friends would make a difference in my life, but the hood has always been with me, drawing me back to my old nature. And good thing! I'm not sure how I could live knowing that my best friend died in my presence and I did nothing, like Eric. I miss my friends, but I had to do this for my boy!

I Can Make It

Well, I'm serving my time now in the big house. If you aren't tough before you get here, this place will make you tough. This is nothing new for me. You see, my rep preceded me, and I am in good company with a few of my old gang partners. The first few months, it took a while for me to network and develop some alliances, but once I did, I had the hook up. It's a whole different world here. I have the crew calling me "Black Jack" and giving me respect.

A few more months go by, and one of the prison guards, a big, burly black man named Mr. Jones, begins to approach me several times daily. He looks intimidating, but I've noticed something different about him. He doesn't look the same way at the inmates as the other guards do. He doesn't even treat us harshly or negatively like the other guards. I suppose it's because he's so big that nobody wants to mess with him. I don't know, but every day he slowly walks up to me and asks if I've read any good books lately and then slowly walks away. It seems like he always walks up to me when I'm thinking about getting into trouble. You know, jailhouse retribution is common. Payback becomes a way of life in the joint if you step across the wrong line—just like the old children's game where you draw a line in the dirt, place a stick on your shoulder, and dare the other person to cross over the line and knock it off.

Almost a year has passed. One day, Mr. Jones stops by my cell and says, "Taylor, I've asked you the same question now every day for months. Have you read any good books lately? I watch you trying to be tough, trying to fit into this environment, trying to live like you are still back on the streets. Let me tell you, son, the only way you can survive the kind of time you have to spend here in the joint is to connect with the right source. Think about it! Go by and see the librarian. Tell him I sent you to get a book. He knows what to give you!"

I figure that he won't stop bothering me until I get this stupid book he keeps talking about. It must be a good book, and what else do I have to do? All I have is time. One day, after months of his persistence, I make a visit to the prison library. The librarian is an older black con who spends his time taking care of the books and occasionally delivering them to the other prisoners. He is quiet, and though I've seen him around several times, I never really paid him any attention. There are a lot of old cons in the joint that just mind their own business and go around really unseen.

"Excuse me," I say. "Mr. Jones, the guard, sent me here to get a book from you. He said you would know what he was talking about."

"Here you are, youngblood!" says the librarian, handing me a copy of the Bible.

"The Bible! What do I need this for? This is supposed to be my 'good' book?" I ask sarcastically.

"Youngblood, this is *the* Good Book! This book will save your life. Have you ever read it before?"

I shake my head. "No!"

"If Mr. Jones sent you to get this, then he is looking out for you, and you should take this and read it. Do you pray?"

Again I shake my head no.

"Okay, take this with you, and come back to see me in about a week or so. I have all the time in the world. We can go over a few things together," the librarian says as he hands me the Bible. He then turns back toward the bookshelves to restock them.

I make sure that I read a little bit at a time every day. I haven't seen Mr. Jones for a couple of weeks, but then out of nowhere, he's standing at my cell one day as I'm reading the Bible.

"I see you've met the librarian. Have you read anything interesting lately?" the guard asks in a direct manner.

"Yes, this Bible talks about love and forgiveness and a bunch of stuff about sin. I know I'm a sinner. I've always been one. I killed a couple of thugs on the street, and now I'm here serving time. The librarian said that reading this will save my life. How?" I ask.

"The librarian holds a study group daily. Go by and tell him that you are ready to join it. You'll learn the answers to your questions there," Mr. Jones says.

"How do you know?" I ask.

"Go see him. He has the answers. He helped me!" Mr. Jones says and then walks away without another word.

The next day, I happen by the prison library and see a group of about ten inmates together in the open area in a circle. The librarian is leading the group in some sort of discussion, and the guard, Mr. Jones, is standing next to the door.

"Come on in and join us, youngblood!" says the librarian.

Although hesitant, I decide to see what's going on out of curiosity. Each of the inmates has a Bible in hand, and the Librarian is conducting a Bible study. He asks me to come in, take a seat, and turn to Matthew 6:14 in my Bible. Of course, I don't have my copy, because, well, just because! I don't just walk around with it. It's private what I do in my cell.

"Here, take one of mine," the librarian says. "Read it for us, please."

I read out loud, "For if you forgive others their trespasses, your heavenly Father will also forgive you" (Matthew 6:14).

"Read what I have written and highlighted in the margin, please," the librarian says.

So I read that out loud too. "It's about my attitude. Forgive because I love the Lord."

I must have a puzzled look on my face, because when I look up from my Bible, everyone has stopped and is looking over at me with smiles on their faces. I turn around, and even the guard is smiling.

"Youngblood and the rest of you, there ain't a sin that God the Father won't forgive, and there ain't a sinner that God the Father doesn't love," he says.

"Youngblood, I'm ashamed to admit it, but I killed a young man out of anger," the librarian says. "Wasn't thinking none at all and just snapped. Before I knew it, I had a knife in my hand and was shoving it in the man. Stabbed him dead just because he stepped on my new pair of shoes. I was about your age then, and now I'm about sixty-five years old. I've been here a long time and found the love of God to keep me safe and secure. You can find him too!" A directness and sense of urgency comes into his voice.

Every one of those hardened criminals looks upward and starts praying. I'm amazed at what I'm witnessing because these are some rough-looking dudes sitting here. I can't believe the peace I'm feeling just watching these cons. Everything the librarian said makes sense to me. It's almost like I've been in a dark room and someone has finally switched the light on. I feel led to confess why I'm in prison. The librarian explains how God's love works and leads me in a prayer of repentance right there on the spot. I can't explain what I'm feeling, but I know that life is about to get better. I've learned that God will forgive anyone, even for the most heinous of sins like killing someone.

Throughout my young life, I never went to church or learned how to pray. I didn't understand the need to trust in God and not myself. I didn't understand about real love. I didn't understand that I needed someone greater than I thought I was, working on my behalf. I'm not quite sure what I really am feeling; I just need to get back to my cell. I don't want to talk to anyone but just go and collect my thoughts.

"Youngblood! Turn it over to the Lord Jesus Christ," the librarian shouts as I hurry out and up to my cell.

That night, in the stillness of my dark prison cell, I fall down on my knees. I talk to God and confess my sins and all the bad things I have done. I can't stop the tears or words from flowing. It's not like any of the other times I've cried; this time I feel a sense of peace and comfort.

The next day, a guard stops me and tells me I have a visitor. It's been months since Mom and Pops last came up to see me, but no one else ever visits, so I know it must be them, since they're back together now. My jaw must have hit the floor when I see behind the glass my girl, Linda. She looks so good and happy. She apologizes for not visiting me before now but says she was really torn up when I dumped her after Kenny's death. I accept her apology and in turn explain why I had to do it. I tell her how being right there when they shot Kenny was more than I could stand. It drove me back to my old gang life, back to my Compton way of thinking. I was so filled with hatred and needed vengeance. Now that I really think about it, I may have wanted it more for me than Kenny.

She understands. I ask her to forgive me. Then she updates me on everything that has gone on and how well she is doing in college. I tell her about my new friends and my experience yesterday and last night.

"I'm a changed man now!" I say in a serious tone.

Linda smiles and says, "Let go and let God."

"What?"

"Stop trying to handle things on your own, because your way obviously doesn't work. Give *all* your questions, problems, and difficulties to God in prayer, and trust in Him to lead you through whatever obstacle you are facing in life."

I nod. "God has changed me, and I believe I can trust Him now. Although I have to live with the consequences, I learned yesterday that He loves me so much that He forgives me of my sins, including murder, if I confess them. I confessed it all last night, and the Lord touched my life and opened up my heart. Things just haven't been the same since." Joy fills my heart.

"Johnny, we can make it together! Hang in there! I'm going to pray and ask God to shorten your sentence. You pray too! I'm glad I came, and I'll be back soon," says Linda.

"Thanks for coming, and I can't wait to see you again," I say.

Even though I am still in the same jail cell for who knows how long, it is no longer dark and lonely. Now it is bright with the Light and love of Jesus. I may physically spend the rest of my life on this earth in prison, but I am happy and at peace because I know that Jesus willingly hung on that cross and died so that my sins may be forgiven. Though I am still incarcerated, I am now truly free! Praise God! With Him all things are truly possible.

Maria's Story Recap

A Homeless Woman's Story

As tears rolled down my face, I thought, *How could I have been so stupid as to fall for this? How could I have been so blinded by love that I did not see the consequences? I did this to myself!*

I had progressed in my drug habit, mixing the pills with alcohol, going day to day with not a care in the world except for my habit. Rico hardly ever came home anymore because he couldn't stand what I had become, barricading myself in my room and not wanting help from anyone, just more drugs.

There was nothing in Rico's office anymore. He had removed the temptation, but the damage was already done. In fact, Rico had realized that he could not afford me sneaking into his product and getting high whenever I felt like it. I guess he decided to move it all to his warehouse and leave nothing more in the house that could cause any more trouble. Or so he thought!

"I need something!" I said to myself as I stumbled to the front door, not caring what I looked like and trying to find someone to help me with a fix.

As I opened the door, my mama and Merissa were standing there getting ready to knock. Surprise! After a long period of worrying and not knowing what was going on with me since I'd left the hospital, they'd decided to get my address from the hospital admittance office since they had no way of contacting me directly. They both were shocked to see the state I was in: drunk, high, and talking abusively toward them. You see, I was so angry with myself that I did not care about anyone else or their feelings.

Mama kept saying to me over and over again, "Maria, we need to pray that Jesus delivers you from these drugs and that alcohol. Jesus will heal you!"

A few moments later, I got so fed up with all the lecturing that I blew up and started cursing at Mama and Merissa. While yelling, I launched my bottle at them and while shaking my fist said, "Never come back here, and take that religious stuff back home with you. I don't want or need it here! All I need is right here in my house with my husband." They hurriedly ran out the door, both crying and speaking in Spanish.

Life has a way of changing what you had in mind, rearranging your dreams, and landing you in the middle of "How did I get here?" I wonder if my expectations were more than my capabilities. I only wanted to be better than the average Latina coming from my background and neighborhood. But here I am ... homeless, husbandless, and hopeless. Hopeless? One would think that by looking at my condition, but I've come a long way over the past year.

"Hey, Mister!" I yell across the street to a passerby. "Hey, Mister!"

As he looks at me, he, like many others, immediately judges me by my appearance, believing me to be a vagrant, a junkie, or both. He begins to walk even faster.

"Hey, Mister, do you know—?" I attempt again.

Before I can get the words completely out of my mouth, the man has turned the corner and is gone out of sight, quite quickly. They always act that way. I didn't want any money or anything else like that. I thought he looked like someone I knew back in the day, someone I went to school with. But I guess he didn't recognize me. Oh, well!

Where did I leave off in my story? Yes, I'm still on the streets—homeless, jobless, penniless, but at least now I have hope! Yes, hope! Not too long ago, I was hopeless and didn't have much to live for, but now I'm happy! I'm content! I'm in control now! There's that look again! You still haven't heard the rest of my story, so let me tell you what happened to me when Rico threw me out of the house.

Picking Up the Broken Pieces

The day that my so-called husband threw me out of my own house, I was suffering from a little problem. He had gotten me hooked on drugs, and because I had a drug habit and drank too, he and a couple of his goons tossed me out on the streets. I was hurting and feeling like my whole world had just been destroyed, and worse yet, I needed a fix badly. I found myself back in the barrio connecting with a few junkies who opened me up to a life of crack cocaine. I was able to stay at the crack house, in my very own corner, inside out of the cold. I never even thought about running home to my mama to let her and my sister see what a failure I had become. The first few days were good, and I didn't have to worry about anything. I had a roof over my head, access to some crack, and food to eat, whenever I was more concerned with eating than smoking. By the end of the week, they told me that I needed money to continue to stay there. Well, let me tell you that I am not proud to admit how I got money to support my habit … I sold my body! I panhandled. I stayed drunk or high so I could do whatever it took to survive back on the streets. I just didn't care!

In just a short while, I had been sexually, physically, and emotionally abused. Some would say that I did what I had to do to survive, day by day. The streets were a mean, filthy place to live. In fact, I had declined into such a state that not much really mattered to me.

One day when I was at my lowest, I ran into Father Clements. I didn't think he would recognize me, but he did.

"Maria? Maria! Is that you?" Father Clements asked as he approached me. "How are you?"

"I'm doing just fine!" I reluctantly answered.

Okay, I was lying, and he could tell I was not fine at all, but that did not stop him from asking me to come inside the church with him. Before I could refuse, he offered me some food and a place to sleep that night. To make a long story short, Father Clements took me to a rehab hospital and made me promise to stay there and let them help me get clean. Several tough weeks later, I came out of the hospital, drug- and alcohol-free. Father Clements came to see me every day, brought me a Bible, and prayed with me. My last couple of weeks there, he even brought my mom by to see me. I was so scared to have to face her after how I'd treated her and Merissa at my house, but they showered me with so much love. We all just cried together.

So you see, my life has changed for the better. But you're probably wondering why I'm still out here on the streets. I can't say my relationship with my momma got better right away, but I now have a very special one with my heavenly Father. I go to Mass every day, and Father Clements reminds me, "Life won't always be easy, but God has always been with you."

Why am I still here? I'm here because I come across so many teenagers and young women like myself who have gone through similar or worse things than I have here on the streets. I tell Father Clements this all the time, and do you know what he says to me? He says, "God has assigned you as an angel, and because they can identify with you, you can help them find their way home."

I know where my home is, and that's why I'm happy and content. Now thank you for listening to me. I hope you understand my story.

Pastor Brown's Story Recap

A Preacher's Story: Where Is Your Faith?

Believing and trusting in God means that despite my circumstances,

131

regardless of my condition, and whether I have it or not, I know that God is a provider and able to do what I cannot. As a Christian, as a man of God, as a pastor, these are basic principles that I know and help others to realize. So why have I allowed my challenges and setbacks to put me exactly where I am now? As these thoughts pour out of me, I find myself in the worst dilemma I have ever faced, and the truth is that I did it to myself. I'm actually stunned at how low I've fallen. I replay in my mind the events that have led me to this crossroads...

"Pastor, as your church treasurer, I need to inform you that the church budget is in the red. We need a new roof, and the congregation would like a new air-conditioning unit put in the sanctuary 'cause the old one is not keeping it cool in there. And, Pastor, we need to cut your salary in order to continue to pay the bills. I'm sorry to be the bearer of this news, but you just need to know. Do you have any ideas?" She looks at me as though she is waiting for some miraculous, save-the-day stroke of wisdom to drop out of the sky into my head and pour out of my mouth.

Actually, I sit there in shock with only the last statement ringing in my head—cut my salary? "Ummm, let me pray about it and get back to you!" I've gotten quite good at saying that so folks won't think I don't know what I'm doing or what to say, even though, to be honest, I don't. As Sister Shirley gets up and leaves, in walks another, and I still haven't had my first cup of coffee yet. All I can think about is an endless parade of trouble.

"Deacon Harris, what can I do for you, sir?" I ask.

"Pastor, I told you I needed to talk to you, before that ole Sister Shirley came running in here blabbing her mouth. I know she told you about the financial problems, and we'll talk about that more later on. I scheduled a meeting for us with the bank to see about another loan."

So to compound the financial problem, instead of relying on God, I decided to take matters in my own hands. I ran into an old buddy, Ray, whom I thought I knew from our childhood days. So in spite of my knowing he had recently been released from prison and that we really hadn't had any contact with each other in years, I accepted an offer that went against my better judgment. Satan had me right where he wanted me because I'd forgotten all about God coming first. I was too eager for a solution, a quick remedy, and didn't involve God, the problem solver.

"Thanks for offering to help me out," I tell Ray. "I need about $50,000, and all our problems will be solved!"

"Sure, church boy," Ray says while laughing and winking at his two associates.

Again I begin to feel a little nervous and ask Ray, "How can we ever repay you?"

It is a rhetorical question, but Ray doesn't let it slip by easily. "Church boy, I'm loaning you this money because that is what we do here. You have ninety days to get it back to me, or we will take whatever collateral we need to fulfill this agreement. Do you understand? This money is yours, so take it and get out of my office. I have other business to attend to, but I'll see you in ninety days!"

As I walk out of the office and the door shuts, I can hear Ray and his two associates laughing. At that moment, I feel as though I've made the biggest mistake ever. I've put my trust in someone who I really barely knew and who has a track record for being on the wrong side of good. Was I a little hasty in my decision? Should I turn around and give him back the money even though I've just told the deacon and Sister Shirley that I have it? I don't want to look like a failure to the church again, but now I don't know what to do.

Prayer Is the Key

I decide to just go back to my church office and do what I should have been doing all the while—*pray*! It's time I activate my faith. I'm trying to do everything on my own and am leaving out God, and the bad part is that I've been acting this way for a while even though I know better. I look up at my daddy's picture, and for a moment, I think he is smiling at me for reassurance.

Again, I hear him whispering in my ear. He says, "Son, don't you remember Jesus and his disciples while out in the middle of the storm? Do you recall what happened to them when everything around them got rough and rocky? Do you recall what He told them?"

My dad always had a way of making sure everything took me back to the Bible. This way I knew it was God speaking directly to my situation. The passage about the boat in the storm:

> Now when He got into a boat, His disciples followed Him. And suddenly a great tempest arose on the sea, so that the boat was covered with the waves. But He was asleep. Then His disciples came to Him and awoke Him, saying, 'Lord, save us! We are perishing!' But He said to them, 'Why are you fearful, O you of little faith?' Then He arose and rebuked the winds and the sea, and there was a great calm.
> (Matthew 8:23-27)

It seems that the more I pray, the more relief and comfort I feel inside of me. My eyes are now open wide to the fact that God has just been waiting on me to turn it over to Him to work it out. The simple fact is that stress never does anything but cause more stress and problems to arise. I had gotten to a place in my life where I had lost the joy of being who God had destined me to be. I was not acting like a pastor to my church and congregation. I was not acting like a father to my children. I was not acting like a husband to my wife. And I certainly was not acting like a child of God prepared to place all my trust in Him. The Devil had messed me up so badly that I'd almost lost my direction.

> Be sober; be vigilant; because your adversary the devil walks about like a roaring lion, seeking whom he may devour.
> (1 Peter 5:8).

As I continue to talk to God, He pours more and more wisdom into me. I feel as if I am a sports player and God is the greatest coach ever and we are about to go against our strongest opponent. He lays out the plan in my head and shows me how to overcome all my problems.

"God, this is great! Yes, I know this will work! All I need to do is execute Your plan and forget about my own. I'm ready when You tell me!" I say with newfound hope.

God Has Our Answer

It's difficult to admit, especially for men, that we don't have all the answers and can't do everything! It's just not possible. In most cases, without God, we wind up messing up the very thing we were determined to do on our own. In other words, our resources and knowledge have limits, but God is infinite in all things. God is our source, and He can meet us just where we are. If we are poor and in need and hold strong to our faith, God can multiply even the smallest thing or amount we have.

I forgot an important principle of God's character. When God tells us He has our needed supply, it is not just a meager amount. God has everything we need. His ability to meet our situation is endless. Faith in Him is the key. Just like the woman who had an encounter with Elisha the prophet. The little oil she thought she had became an abundant supply because of her obedience:

> A certain woman of the wives of the sons of the prophets cried out to Elisha, saying, "Your servant my husband is dead, and you know that your servant feared the Lord. And the creditor is coming to take my two sons to be his slaves." So Elisha said to her, "What shall I do for you? Tell me, what do you have in the house?" And she said, "Your maidservant has nothing in the house but a jar of oil." Then he said, "Go, borrow vessels from everywhere, from all your neighbors—empty vessels; do not gather just a few. And when you have come in, you shall shut the door behind you and your sons; then pour it into all those vessels, and set aside the full ones." So she went from him and shut the door behind her and her sons, who brought the vessels to her; and she poured it out. Now it came to pass, when the vessels were full, that she said to her son, "Bring me another vessel." And he said to her, "There is not another vessel." So the oil ceased. Then she came and told the man of God. And he said, "Go, sell the oil and pay your debt; and you and your sons live on the rest. (2 Kings 4:1-7)

"God, I'm ready to believe that what You did for her can happen for us. I believe it and count it as done. Let's get everything back on track, Your way," I say while looking both upward toward God and at my dad's picture. Maybe I need glasses; I think my dad smiled at me again.

I pick up the phone and call our bank loan representative and ask if he can come to the church for a 3:00 p.m. meeting with the church officials to figure out what we can do to get a loan sufficient to eliminate our problems. He agrees. I then call Deacon Harris and ask him to have the trustees and deacons all here at 3:00 p.m. to meet concerning our financial needs. He agrees. Everything is working as God outlined for me. Now the final important element of the plan—Ray! One last phone call and now Ray is on board to come to the called meeting at 3:00 p.m. I am so happy this portion of the plan has worked perfectly; now on to the best part of it.

As everyone sits at the conference table, I think, *Wow, look at God work!* As Mr. Epstein, from the bank, passes out the financial ledgers and criteria necessary to obtain the loan, the only one missing is Ray. At that moment, Ray walks in with a couple of his so-called associates.

"Brother Ray, glad you could make it," I say. "This is Mr. Epstein from the bank. Please take a seat. We are getting ready to review our church expansion options and need for the loan. The bank refused us before, because we did not have the sufficient cash to show we have the ability to repay such a sizable loan amount."

Ray has a puzzled look on his face. I can tell he's not really sure why he is here, but he starts reading through the paperwork in front of him. Mr. Epstein finishes his presentation, and I ask everyone at the table to sign a document I got earlier from the bank. I had advised Mr. Epstein that he did not need to discuss it and that we would all sign at the end. After we all sign, I stand, look at Ray and Mr. Epstein, and say, "I want to thank you gentlemen for taking time out of your busy schedules to help us sort out the final pieces for this church renovation project. Since we only needed a small percentage of the money that you have already invested in us, Brother Ray, now with your signature on the declaration paperwork from the bank, we will be able to begin this process immediately. Mr. Epstein, if you have any questions or concerns, please feel free to contact our new trustee, Brother Ray. He will make sure that all requirements are met according to the bank's guidelines, since thanks to him, his businesses will be our source of collateral."

All the other church board members are overjoyed with this new development. Deacon Harris smiles from ear to ear. As Mr. Epstein gathers his belongings, he once again congratulates everyone and then leaves. The board members, in turn, also leave. I remain sitting and look over at Ray, who is literally in shock.

He shakes his head in wonderment and asks, "Church boy, what kind of game did you just run on me? Did you just outslick me?"

"No, Ray, God knew you wanted to help the church, and this way, you can receive the rightful recognition for your gracious donation of $10,000. Here is the remaining $40,000 and if you still demand the other back, we will, but over time and on our own terms. Agreed?"

Ray reluctantly shakes his head "Yes" and then smiles feeling he is now a part of the community again. He doing something that will make him more respectable, not just an ex-con.

"Now, I expect to see you every Sunday to observe what good use your money is being put to. And of course, your friends are invited to come back too."

As all three get up and leave the room, again I'm almost certain that I hear my dad and God both laughing and celebrating our victory together. I look over at my dad's picture and say, "I've learned my lesson, and from this day forward, things will be much different for me. God, thank You for not giving up on me and putting me back on the right track. I promise to uphold my calling to the fullest now. I will be the leader of this church and of my home. From now on, God, You first in everything we do!"

I hurry home, gather my family, and take them out for dinner. Over dinner, I explain to them how I allowed too many things to get in the way of my time with my family and say that I will never allow that to happen again.

I say, "From now on, I promise that you are my priority! God has shown me a better way to be faithful to everyone, including Him. I love you all, and I have a lot of missed time to make up for, if you forgive me?"

The next day, I hold a huge church meeting. I take this opportunity to inform the congregation that the church has received a large donation to conduct some major renovations and expansion of the church. The congregation erupts in shouts and applause. I then outline the plan as given to me by God and explain what needs to be done, as a church, to continue forward. Again the congregation applauds with several members shouting, "Amen, Pastor!"

Finally, I look out at my family and then to the leadership sitting in the front and say, "Oh yes, and I'm not going anywhere. We can do this together if everyone has faith to believe! We have the loan. We have the plan and vision according to God. With God for us, who can be against us? Are you with me? Who's ready to trust in God like me?"

Another major eruption of applause and shouts explodes all over the church. It is the largest celebration since I became pastor here. As Mother King and Sister Shirley wave their hands in joyous agreement, I can feel the presence of my dad and God joining me in the pulpit, patting me on my back and saying, "Well done!"

Oh, I see that from now on, we're going to have some brighter days here at Glory Gate Holiness Missionary Baptist Church.

"Come on, church, let's sing 'Oh Happy Day'!"

Reflective Key Verse

> Blessed is the man who endures temptation: for when he has been approved, he will receive the crown of life which the Lord has promised to those who love Him.

—James 1:12

Spiritual Moment

In this passage of Scripture, James is writing to people who are going through some hard times and struggling to survive. They are Christians and are trying to live trusting Christ in spite of their difficulties. How then should they go through their trials as Christians? James returns to the thought with which he began his letter: "Blessed is the man who endures trial, for when he has stood the test he will receive the crown of life which God has promised to those who love him." How do you feel blessed when you're in the storm? How do you feel blessed when you're being burnt by the fire?

James reminds us that to endure, like counting it all joy, is not something that we do by sheer will power. To endure is to continue to turn to God as our only source of life. It is to count on Him to give us His presence and His peace in the midst of whatever we are facing. And it is to live knowing that God is bringing us through our current situation. So additionally, James states here that we should "endure temptation."

James further states that going ahead and being deceived by temptation now has consequences that go beyond our control. Our actions can eventually lead us to death. It's so easy to take lightly our little sins. We fail to see where they will lead us.

Life Challenge

When we are in a trial, we are tempted to doubt God's Word and to take matters into our own hands. Observe Rick, Johnny, Maria, and Pastor Brown; each was tempted to find meaning, purpose, identity, and life elsewhere and in other things, outside of the will of God. God's purpose in allowing trials and temptations in our lives is to show us that it is in Him that we can truly trust. God did not put you here with the express purpose of seeking personal happiness. His desire is for your holiness and trust in Him who created us to be different from the world.

CHAPTER 8

What Will It Be: Life or Death

"For I know the thoughts that I think toward you, says
the Lord, thoughts of peace and not of evil, to give you a
future and a hope.

—Jeremiah 29:11

Finding Purpose in Life

Any of these characters, individually or in combination, could
represent any one of us. None of us, as Christians, are too blessed to
remember that whatever our situation may be now, we could have easily
fallen in the same pit of disaster as Rick, Marie, Johnny, or Pastor Brown.
In fact, maybe your story is more desperate, more heartbreaking, more
tear-jerking, but I must say that the final analysis isn't in the "*was*" but in
the "*now*." It's in the "Look where God has brought me or delivered me
from." Will you be ready when the Lord Jesus comes back to reclaim His
own? What will it be: eternal life or eternal death? Or more simply put,

would you rather spend your eternity in heaven or eternal damnation in hell? And let me just set the record straight; according to the Bible, there is a big difference, and both are real. Allow me to help you, whoever you may be, make a decision.

Believers and nonbelievers alike, consciously or subconsciously, have faith or trust in something. You have faith or trust in the fact that as sure as you were born, someday, your time in this world will come to an end. Paul wrote, "But as it is written: Eye has not seen, nor ear heard, nor have entered into the heart of man the things which God has prepared for those who love Him" (1 Corinthians 2:9).

Through the creativity of the mind, we can imagine and vividly express an interpretation of what we think heaven and hell are like. Many of us have either read countless books or seen several movies made to tantalize our mental awareness of heaven and hell.

Our everyday language is heavily laced with statements of faith that we make without even thinking. Whatever else this phenomenon may mean, it cannot be denied that heaven and hell have been set in the minds of both believers and nonbelievers as a placeholder of things to come.

Here is where, as an ordained preacher, I want to prepare you for in terms of the finality of this life. As I am not an eyewitness and have never in all my travels been to either place, let me share scripturally, so you have a reference point for your own analysis. True love shows how much one cares by his or her actions.

A Place Called Heaven

The apostle John, who shares as an eyewitness in the book of Revelation, the last book of the Bible, dramatically gives us a visual

Picasso of heaven as having streets of pure gold, gates of pearl, and walls decorated with every manner of precious gemstones.

> Also she had a great and high wall with twelve gates, and twelve angels at the gates, and names written on them, which are the names of the twelve tribes of the children of Israel: three gates on the east, three gates on the north, three gates on the south, and three gates on the west. Now the wall of the city had twelve foundations, and on them were the names of the twelve apostles of the Lamb. And he who talked with me had a gold reed to measure the city, its gates, and its wall. The city is laid out as a square; its length is as great as its breadth. And he measured the city with the reed: twelve thousand furlongs. Its length, breadth, and height are equal. Then he measured its wall: one hundred and forty-four cubits, according to the measure of a man, that is, of an angel. The construction of its wall was of jasper; and the city was pure gold, like clear glass. The foundations of the wall of the city were adorned with all kinds of precious stones: the first foundation was jasper, the second sapphire, the third chalcedony, the fourth emerald, the fifth sardonyx, the sixth sardius, the seventh chrysolite, the eighth beryl, the ninth topaz, the tenth chrysoprase, the eleventh jacinth, and the twelfth amethyst. The twelve gates were twelve pearls: each individual gate was of one pearl. And the street of the city was pure gold, like transparent glass. (Revelation 21:12–21)

The Bible says that nothing impure ever will be in heaven, and the residents shall live eternally in the presence of God and Jesus Christ. This is a place where the righteous shall go for eternity. It is a place of joy, peace, and love. Jesus Himself has prepared a wonderful place for us.

Let not your heart be troubled; you believe in God, believe also in Me. In My Father's house are many mansions; if *it were* not *so*, I would have told you. I go to prepare a place for you. And if I go and prepare a place for you, I will come again and receive you to Myself; that where I am, *there* you may be also. And where I go you know, and the way you know. (John 14:1-4)

Heaven is the kingdom of God. It is a place of unspeakable glory where the elect of God live with one another in the immediate presence of God and Jesus Christ. It is a place where the curse of sin and all of its effects have been removed forever from all who dwell there; they, being made joint heirs with Christ, will inherit all things and live without the troubles, heartaches, pains, trials, tribulations, hatred, and melancholy of this world. All that live there dwell in a state of perfect happiness and joy forever. We are told that God has prepared a city for the righteous, and we are given a preview of the glory of this city in the book of Revelation, chapter 21.

It is also a place that remains forever. It is called "eternal" or "everlasting," and of its inhabitants it is said, "neither can they die anymore, for they are like the angels, and are sons of God" (Luke 20:36). Those who go to heaven live in that glorious city for all eternity. It will be like paradise. While on the cross next to Jesus Christ, a thief, who was also being crucified, recognized Jesus as his Lord and Savior and made a startling request: "Then he said to Jesus, 'Lord, remember me when You come into Your kingdom!'" (Luke 23:42). Jesus responded, "Truly I tell you, today you will be with Me in paradise" (Luke 23:43, NIV). Jesus calls heaven "Paradise." We often refer to an exotic, tropical island as *paradise*, yet this heavenly paradise will make all earthly paradises look meager and barren.

In heaven, unhindered love shall flow forth to God as none have ever experienced on earth. God shall be loved completely and fully, and the saints shall love one another without carnality or selfishness being present. "In Your presence is fullness of joy; At Your right hand are pleasures forevermore" (Psalm 16:11). The seeing of God, loving God, and being beloved of God will cause a jubilation of our spirits and create that unspeakable holy rapture of joy. The psalmist wrote of the great blessing attending the worship of God in His temple: "Blessed are those who dwell in Your house; They will still be praising You. For the Lord God is a sun and shield; the Lord will give grace and glory; no good thing will He withhold from those who walk uprightly" (Psalm 84:4, 11).

Lastly, Heaven is the place where sin will be no more. This is depicted beautifully in Revelation 21:3–4: "And God Himself will be with them and be their God. And God will wipe away every tear from their eyes; there shall be no more death, nor sorrow, nor crying. There shall be no more pain, for the former things have passed away."

Why are there tears? Why is there death? Why do we mourn, cry, and feel pain? It is all because of sin. Sin brings all those evils upon us. In heaven, we will be free from sin and the three primary causes of sin: our sinful nature, the temptations of the Devil, and the lure of the world. Our sinful nature is the source of the sins that we commit. The Bible tells us: "Each one is tempted when he is drawn away by his own desires and enticed. Then, when desire has conceived, it gives birth to sin" (James 1:14–15a). "For I know that in me (that is, in my flesh) nothing good dwells" (Romans 7:18a).

In heaven, your fleshly body shall be made like unto His glorious body, and you will no longer know sin. You will not be subject to the daily assaults and drawn into temptation by the devil. You will no longer be subject to the desires of this world. You will be free from the consequences of sin. The primary consequence of sin is eternal punishment in hell. Scripture makes it clear that a person at death goes to either heaven or hell. There is no in-between state or place, no purgatory, no other option. Those who go to heaven are spared the wrath of God, which falls upon those in hell. They are delivered from "the wrath to come" (1 Thessalonians 1:10). Physical death, which opens the door into eternity, is also one of the consequences of sin. Death came originally as a direct penal infliction upon man because of his sin: "The sting of death is sin" (1 Corinthians 15:56), "but thanks be to God, who gives us the victory through our Lord Jesus Christ. Death is swallowed up in victory" so that the child of God can boldly say, "Oh, death where is your victory? O death, where is your sting?" (1 Corinthians 15:54, 55, 57).

The Other Place Called Hell

Hell, on the other hand, is described as a "lake of fire" (Revelation 20:15), "the second death" (Revelation 21:8), "a place where there will be weeping and gnashing of teeth" (Luke 13:28), "the home of the wicked" (Psalm 9:17 NIV), and "a place of torment" (Revelation 20:10). Hell is where those who reject the great sacrifice of Jesus will spend eternity.

How many times have you heard someone declare the nonexistence of hell? How about believers saying that they are tired of coming to certain churches and always hearing those fire-and-brimstone-type messages? I've even been told by other pastors that their people don't want to hear the gloom and doom of eternal death and hell. Hello! Let me just interject the reality of this place to those who may be in a state of confusion. Actually, you should be in a state of fear because of the reality of this place.

When hell is mentioned today, it is generally glossed over or ridiculed, as if the whole idea of hell is so old-fashioned that only the naive and ignorant would really believe that such a place actually exists. People live their lives thinking that maybe if they ignore a difficulty long enough, it will go away. There has also been some newly misconceived doctrine discounting the reality of hell. Why should we be so concerned about hell? Why should we spend time reading about hell? There are several reasons why it is profitable to do so: most importantly, we should do so because the Bible speaks of it as a real place!

> "So it will be at the end of the age; the angels will come forth, separate the wicked from among the just, and cast them into the furnace of fire. There shall be wailing and gnashing of teeth" (Matthew 13:49–50).

Hell is described as a furnace of unquenchable fire, a place of everlasting punishment, where its victims are tormented in both their bodies and their minds in accordance with their sinful natures, their actual sins committed, and the amount of spiritual light given to them, which they rejected. Hell is a place from which God's mercy and goodness have been withdrawn, where God's wrath is revealed as a terrifying, consuming fire, and people live with unfulfilled lusts and desires in torment forever and ever.

In examining these words of the Lord Jesus, we should first notice that hell is described as being a furnace of fire. Nebuchadnezzar's furnace was heated seven times hotter than normal and is described as "a furnace of blazing fire" (Daniel 3:23). John the Baptist spoke of "unquenchable fire," and Revelation describes hell as "a lake of fire burning with brimstone" (Revelation 19:20). Imagine every part of your body on fire at the same time, so that every fiber of your being feels the intense torment of being burned. How long could you endure such punishment? Christ tells us that "there shall be wailing and gnashing of teeth." The lost will endure the most intense pain and suffering they have ever felt as the flames consume them and constantly burn every part of their bodies. And there will be no relief.

Hell is also described as a place of darkness. Jude writes of those in hell "for whom the black darkness has been reserved forever" (Jude v. 13). In Luke 16:19–26, Christ tells us of two men. One of them was rich, and the other, Lazarus, was poor. Both men died. The poor man was carried by angels to heaven, and the rich man went to hell. The rich man did not go to hell because he was rich, nor did the poor man go to heaven simply because he was poor.

The Lord shows us through this contrast that our circumstances may change drastically when we pass from time into eternity. God may not have dealt harshly with us here, but we should not be fooled into thinking that he will not do so after death. The eternal place of both men resulted from the condition of their hearts before God while they were on earth. Lazarus was a true follower of God. The rich man was not. Luke 16:23–24 indicate that the rich man is "in torment."

What does it mean to be "in torment"? This torment refers to both torment in body and torment in soul as well. The sinners' bodies will be tormented in a furnace of fire. Every part of the body will feel the pain of that fire. Death from cancer is sometimes said to cause extreme pain in the body, but the pain of hell will be far worse. If your body were afflicted with many different and painful diseases all at the same time, you still would not begin to approach the pain levels of those people cast into hell. They will never find any resting place there, any secret corner that is cooler than the rest, where they may have a little respite, a small abatement of the extremity of their torment. They never will be able to find any cooling stream or fountain in any part of that world of torment; no, they won't find as much as a drop of water to cool their tongues. They will find no company to give them any comfort or do them the least good. They will find no place where they can remain, rest, and take breath for one minute, for they will be tormented with fire and brimstone and will have no rest day or night forever and ever.

There seems to be a real lack of fear today of the reality of hell. This applies to both those in the church and those in the world. People are not afraid of hell. Why? We hear of hell in the Bible. We know that the Lord Jesus spoke of hell. In fact, Jesus spoke more of hell than anyone else in the Scriptures. Why do people not believe hell is real? Well, it's because they do not hear enough about it. We don't study what the Scriptures say about hell. In addition to what we hear, what we do *not* hear helps to form our belief systems. Only the Spirit of God can make the realities of hell present to us.

The doctrine of hell has been used by God more often to the conversion of sinners than any other doctrine in the Scriptures. Pray now that as you read this chapter, the Holy Spirit will set hell before you as real indeed. Hell is necessary because of the condition of the heart (Jeremiah 17:9) and is eternal. That means it is forever. It's like a prisoner who has been sentenced to multiple life terms. You're put in a place where there is no escape, and when you die, you have to come right back! Your mind cannot conceive of eternity, but it is nonetheless real. Let's look at the Scriptures:

> The devil who deceived them was thrown into the lake of
> fire and brimstone, where the beast and the false prophet
> are also; and they will be tormented day and night
> forever and ever. (Revelation 20:10).

Hell is forever and ever. How could a stronger, more certain expression be used? Imagine yourself cast into a fiery oven or a great furnace, where your pain would be much greater than that occasioned by accidentally touching a coal of fire, as the heat is greater. Imagine also that your body is to lie there for a quarter of an hour, full of fire, and all the while full of quick sense; what desperation would you feel at the entrance of such a furnace? And how long would that quarter of an hour seem to you? And after you had endured it for one minute, how overbearing would it be to you to think that you had to endure the other fourteen? But what would be the effect on your soul if you knew you must endure that torment to the fullest for twenty-four hours… for a whole year… for a thousand years? Oh, then how would your heart sink if you knew that you must bear it forever and ever? But your torment in hell will be immensely greater than this illustration represents.

Charles Haddon Spurgeon said, "In Hell, there is no hope. They have not even the hope of dying—the hope of being annihilated. They are forever lost! On every chain in Hell, there is written 'forever.' In the fires, flames blaze out the words, 'forever.' Above their heads, they read, 'forever.' Their eyes are galled, and their hearts are pained with the thought that it is 'forever.'"

How to Choose—Life

God has given us the ability to choose between right and wrong, good, and bad, do and don't. There are so many options in life but making the wrong choices can determine the way our eternity plays out. Whether you're a believer or nonbeliever, the truth is that we all have experiences in life that have affected us. So even though you have a choice, God makes it clear that your choices can incur a penalty. "For the wages of sin is death, but the gift of God is eternal life in Christ Jesus our Lord" (Romans 6:23).

Listen, the cost for you committing an act (sin) that is not of God is death. Sin is your real enemy. Sin is worse than hell because sin gave birth to hell. Would you be willing to go to hell for all eternity for the enjoyment of a little pleasure and disobedience to God here on earth? Flee from sin! Flee from living for self and self-pleasing to Jesus Christ. When you die, it will be too late. All opportunity to repent ends at death. I cannot leave without one final word to those who think they are converted but are not and to those who know themselves to be unconverted. Can you conceive of eternity? Stop now, and try to imagine being tormented unceasingly, forever, without end. Does this not terrify you? There is never a chance for a moment's rest. There is never a drop of water to cool your parched throat. Think again of how long eternity is. Try to imagine it: day and night, forever and ever, burned with fire in a furnace of flames. Shrieking, howling, wailing, cursing the day you were born, and being cursed by the Devil and other souls just like you, all around you, eternally. Forever remembering how you were warned on numerous occasions, including right now, and how you ignored those warnings: self-satisfied and self-deceived that all was well with your soul. Unless you repent and flee to Jesus Christ, who is your only hope, you shall be tormented eternally, and you shall never die. You shall feel pain and anguish. You shall feel burning. You shall never die! And the worst part of it is that eternity is forever!

Today is the day that you must decide for yourself and make up your mind. Today is the day that after reading this book, you decide which path in life to travel. Today is the day when you can stand up and shout, "It could have been me, but I'm so glad Jesus Christ came into my life and made the difference... forever!"

Reflective Key Verse

For I know the thoughts that I think toward you, says the Lord, thoughts of peace and not of evil, to give you a future and a hope.

—Jeremiah 29:11

Spiritual Moment

In chapter 29 of the book of Jeremiah, the Weeping Prophet delivers a message from God to the children of Israel held in captivity by the Babylonians, contradicting the misleading claims by false prophets. Jeremiah 29:11 presents proof from God that He has a wonderful future in store for us. That word "*future*" used in Jeremiah 29:11 can be translated as an "expected end." Another translation could say "things hoped for" or "outcome."

It's easy when thinking about God's plan for our lives to have the attitude "it's all about me." Yes, it's true that God cares about every intricate detail in our lives. In fact, Jesus said that even the hairs on our heads are numbered. The problem we encounter today is that it's so easy for us to mistakenly think that God's plan is always going to be a feel-good plan with the intent to make us happy. Let me pause to say that God is more concerned about your holiness than your happiness.

Jeremiah, in this passage of Scripture, is writing to a group of people in exile from their homeland who are being held captive. He's writing to let them know that although they're not where they would have expected or where they would have asked God to place them, God has not forgotten them and still has a plan for their lives. Even in the midst of a difficult situation, God wants them to know His plans. In the preceding verses we see that a big part of God's plan is for them to "seek the peace of the city where I have caused you to be carried away captive, and pray to the Lord for it; for in its peace you will have peace" (Jeremiah 29:7). In other words, God wants them to know that His plans are not just to benefit them personally. God is also telling them that He's not removing them from the situation immediately. He does promise to eventually restore them, but it's not coming quickly (seventy years out when many of them will be dead). God is letting them know they can move forward, because in the eternal picture, God's justice will prevail and everything will even out.

Today, in the midst of difficult situations, God wants us to know He has a plan. He also wants us to know that as we submit to His plan, He desires to use us to bless the world around us. The key still remains during both good and difficult times: "And *you will seek Me [God] and find Me, when you search for Me with all your heart.*" (Jeremiah 29:13)

Life Challenge

At this moment, I may not know what God has in mind for me. But He knows. The way God understands the future and how we understand the future is much like an artist's understanding of a blank canvas and our understanding of a blank canvas. The artist looks at the white canvas and paces back and forth. He takes out a pencil and draws a couple of broad strokes and then looks at it again. Then we walk up and say, "What is that?" He tells us, and we respond, "Well, it doesn't look like that to us." But the artist confidently remarks, "It's coming! It's a work in progress! I have a vision, a plan!" The artist is thinking about the end result even though he has drawn only a couple of seemingly meaningless strokes. His vision far exceeds what we think.

We oftentimes look at our unfinished lives in the same way we might look at a blank canvas. Things may not be going as expected. Life is not progressing according to our schedules. So we say, "The Lord must have forgotten about me. The Lord has abandoned me. It's over." No! The Lord has a vision for your life. He has a plan. You are a work in progress. You are under construction. God is not finished with you yet. Stay in the hands of the Master, and He will continue to mold you and give you purpose.

CHAPTER 9

Don't Quit...Keep Moving!

But those who wait on the Lord Shall renew *their* strength; They shall mount up with wings like eagles, They shall run and not be weary, They shall walk and not faint

—Isaiah 40:31

Sign of the Times

There are so many colloquial phrases and words being used these days to express a sign of the times. Many of these come directly to us via the television ... live, horrific, and stunning. Too many times, we become so immersed in tragedy and declining situations worldwide that we just shrug our shoulders and market it as "a sign of the times." Each passing generation has looked upon the younger generation and labeled them with some oddity or mishap that never would have occurred during their generation. It's as if each generation has become the duty watch officer, and their proclamation is that the events or circumstances did not occur during their watch! However, history continues to reveal and play forward a crisis act or troubled society that seems to only worsen as time goes by because we hide away or ignore the situation, thinking that it will just go away and get better. Guess what: there is no getting better until we make it that way and do the right things to prevent the mishaps that only build on previous avoidance. Today, we have more teenage pregnancies, more young people killing one another, more violence everywhere, more drug abuse, more heinous crimes, more poverty, more homeless families, more jail sentences for children, and the list goes on ... more, more, more. There is no getting better until we make it that way through the love of God.

Sign of the times is not just some simple phrase. It should be a jeering wake-up call to everyone. Let me say this! It does not take a genius or theologian to see that this world is changing daily and that events occurring across the globe are making history. *Sign of the times* is not just some pretty title for songs talking about what is going on throughout the world. The phrase is an indicator that time is winding down for the wickedness that prevails in this world. And as history repeats itself, the conditions and issues seem to be more devastating than before. Biblically, the sign of the times marks the end of days. However, the time is still a mystery known only by God, so these signs signal to us that it's time to get ready and prepare ourselves.

Our Only True Security

As I write these words, it's too early to tell where the current economic situation will lead. There is a paramount truth in the fact that the things of this world are fleeting, uncertain, and fragile. We've just seen fortunes vanish overnight. How true are the words of John? "For everything in the world—the lust of the flesh, the lust of the eyes, and the pride of life—comes not from the Father but from the world" (1 John 2:16).

Yes, the things of this world—be they money, position, power, even our health—are fleeting and transitory and will pass away. The good news, however, is that the same Bible that warns of the fall of Babylon also tells of another city, the New Jerusalem.

The apostle John said, "I saw the Holy City, the new Jerusalem, coming down out of heaven from God, prepared as a bride beautifully dressed for her husband. And I heard a loud voice from the throne saying, 'Look! God's dwelling place is now among the people, and he will dwell with them. They will be his people, and God himself will be with them and be their God. He will wipe every tear from their eyes. There will be no more death or mourning or crying or pain, for the old order of things has passed away'" (Revelation 21:2–4 NIV).

This Scripture is food for thought if you're still on the edge concerning your decision to choose eternal life. Jesus came down from glory, bore our sins on the cross, and died for us; but in rising from the grave, He offers every person a chance to live in this New Jerusalem, where the toils, trials, and tragedies of Babylon will forever be a thing of the past.

In this life and while we are still part of this world, we face obstacles and situations that whisper into our ears, "Give up and quit." Have you ever been tempted to quit anything? Most employees, stuck on the nine-to-five roller coaster, dread coming back to work after the weekend. If you ask them, "How often do you feel that way?" they may say, "Most every Monday." Don't ever get tricked into quitting on life! There is normally a no-escape clause tied to quitting.

Let's examine the events that occurred in the book of Exodus as an illustration of this situation, specifically the events of chapter 5. This chapter occurs after God called Moses at the burning bush. Moses had already gone through his many objections as to why he should not return to Egypt to lead Israel out, and now he was convinced that he had the responsibility. Therefore, he returned to Egypt where he met with the leaders of Israel. Consider these words: "Moses and Aaron brought together all the elders of the Israelites, and Aaron told them everything the Lord had said to Moses. He also performed the signs before the people, and they believed. And when they heard that the Lord was concerned about them and had seen their misery, they bowed down and worshiped." (Exodus 4:29-31 NIV)

Now those are encouraging words. Moses and Aaron came back. They met with the leaders of Israel. In essence, they said, "God appeared to us. Look at the signs." To which the leaders of the people responded, "Yes! We're out of here. Let's worship God." Things were looking good. If only they had stayed that way. Such was not the case, however. Moses went to talk with Pharaoh. He said, "God has appeared, and He says, 'Let My people go!'" To this Pharaoh replied in essence, "Not on your life." Pharaoh continued, "Obviously, things are too easy for you lazy Israelites. Therefore, we will make it tougher on you." And Pharaoh did. No longer did they supply straw for making bricks, but the tally of the bricks remained exactly the same. Instead of circumstances getting better and easier, instead of being released from bondage to go and worship God, the whole situation worsened.

After this had gone on for some time, the Israelite foremen left Pharaoh "and found Moses and Aaron waiting to meet them. They said, 'May the Lord look upon you and judge you! You have made us a stench to Pharaoh and his officials and have put a sword in their hand to kill us'" (Exodus 5:20–21 NIV).

These were the same leaders who had been so excited just a short time before. These were the people who had been worshiping the Lord, who had been thankful when everything looked so good. Observe the 180-degree change. These same people, who were so excited, so joyous at the end of Exodus 4, are now ready to get rid of Moses at the end of Exodus 5.

How does Moses respond to this shocking change in their attitude and words? "So Moses returned to the Lord and said, 'Lord, why have You brought trouble on this people? Why is it You have sent me? For since I came to Pharaoh to speak in Your name, he has done evil to this people; neither have You delivered Your people at all'" (Exodus 5:22–23).

In Moses' mind, this whole problem is God's fault. I can imagine Moses say, "Lord, why did You do this to me? You brought me here, and it did not work." I can picture Moses crying out to God and saying the same kind of words that you and I have thought and maybe also said. "All right, God, just give me three good reasons why I shouldn't quit." And so God does. And whatever you're facing, God is giving you a reason also not to quit!

Keep Pressing

Like Moses and like Rick, Johnny, Maria, and Pastor Brown, we sometimes come to junctures in life when reality is hitting us hard and we must make serious decisions but don't know what to do. We think, I can't take any more. How much does God expect me to bear? Why doesn't He help me?

Have you ever felt like this? Job pressures, family problems, church troubles, health issues, relational conflicts, and financial struggles—the list of overwhelming difficulties is endless. It's hard to see a light at the end of a dark tunnel, let alone comprehend how you could possibly walk toward it victoriously. Where can you find the strength to keep going

161

when you're so weary? Thankfully, God gives us an amazing promise: "But those who wait on the Lord shall renew their strength; They shall mount up with wings like eagles, They shall run and not be weary, They shall walk and not faint" (Isaiah 40:31).

This verse isn't just about physical weakness. Emotional exhaustion can be even more draining. When we're worn out, a good night's sleep will usually renew our strength, but emotional weariness can utterly deplete us. Then fears and doubts rush in: *How will I ever deal with tomorrow? God, where are You?*

That's exactly how the Israelites felt when the Lord spoke through the prophet Isaiah: "Why do you say, O Jacob, and speak, O Israel, 'My way is hidden from the Lord, and my just claim is passed over by my God" (Isaiah 40:27). Sometimes our circumstances make us feel that the Lord has forgotten all about us. This attitude indicates we've forgotten that suffering and hardship are a part of life—even for believers. The key to victory in hardships is not quitting, surrendering, or planning our own escape. Anyone can keep going when burdens are removed, but those who trust in the Lord in the midst of difficulties will persevere.

While we see only our immediate needs, God has already predestined us with a plan outlining the eternal perspective of our situation. Because He created us (Genesis 1:26–27; 2:7), He's made plans for our lives (Jeremiah 29:11), and with each passing day filled with circumstances and events, He is working out these plans. Now, since we don't know the end result, we become detoured by selfish ideals. God never loses track of us and always has our best interest in mind. God's reasons for allowing tests and trials to come into our lives may be beyond our comprehension, but they're always designed to help us fulfill God's desired outcome. If you've ever been tempted to give up or complain to the Lord, perhaps you don't understand how much God wants to help you. Everything we do and encounter in life is based on God's will. God knows us, and because He knows us, He knows how much we can bear, how long we can bear it, and the perfect time to provide divine support. "No temptation has seized you except what is common to man. And God is faithful; he will not let you be tempted beyond what you can bear. But when you are tempted, he will also provide a way out so that you can stand up under it" (1 Corinthians 10:13).

Just look at God! He is a burden bearer and heavy-load sharer. He will never put more on us than we can bear, but what He allows strengthens us to proceed to the next level with the ability to persevere through whatever comes our way. It's all part of the plan. In addition to helping us individually, our faithfulness to Him as we go through trials can help others who are facing the same things we've been through. We become a living testimony to His provisions.

"He gives strength to the weary and to him who lacks might He increases power" (Isaiah 40:29). God never intends that we live out of our own strength. Whether you are in need of physical or emotional might, He can replenish you with His divine energy. Isaiah tells us that the key is to "wait for the Lord" (Isaiah 40:31). That's probably the last thing you want to hear when you're burdened and overwhelmed. You want relief, not delays! How do you rise above the obstacles in your life? Wait on the Lord! However, waiting for the Lord is not the same as waiting for the end of a difficult season in life.

The Hebrew word that translates to "wait" carries with it the idea of hope and expectation. Since we don't automatically know what to expect from God or how He's going to work in our lives, we need to spend time with Him, share how we feel through prayer, and then direct our full attention toward the Scriptures to understand what He desires to accomplish in and through us. Then we should quietly listen in anticipation of His answer. As we rely on His promises, our anxiety will be replaced with His peace.

This is exactly what we all need, including Rick, Johnny, Maria, and Pastor Brown. In time, God will show us what He intends for us, but the lesson may come as a bitter pill to swallow and may be learned through failure. If you've been a Christian or in ministry for some time, you start to believe that you'll always walk in the favor of God, even when God has provided specific instructions for you and you've decided to veer another way. You begin to think that God and you can accomplish anything, and you pour a large amount of yourself into doing something that God doesn't support. What we fail to realize is that we begin running according to our own plans and in our own power, not His. Once that occurs, God will eventually sideline you. In other words, He will basically put you in a spiritual time-out to get your attention. And during that time, we must recognize that we can't expect to plot our own course, thinking God will come alongside to help if we get in a mess. He gives strength for the burdens He allows, not for the ones we take upon ourselves apart from His will. The only way to keep going in hard times is to let Christ live through us. When we come to the end of ourselves and accept the truth, that He will sustain us no matter what, we can accomplish whatever we're called to do. The Lord never promises to shield us from challenges, but we can be confident that if we have to run, He'll strengthen us as we go. And if the journey is long, He'll help us walk through it without losing heart. When we wait upon Him, believing that He is able and willing to come to our aid, anything is possible. That's the beauty of the good news.

Again, picture this and say with me, "It could have been me—in a wheelchair or laid up in a hospital bed with no one to help me get where I need to go. It could have been me—living on the streets and pushing a cart struggling to find food, clothing, and shelter. It could have been me—pregnant as a teenager and contemplating dropping out of school with no father for the child in sight. It could have been me—selling my body just to live only to discover I've contracted a big disease with a little name."

I could go on and on until I reached into your personal closet and pulled out something that fit you—drug addiction, alcohol abuse, violence, jail time, and so on. Possibly, any one of these could have been you or me, but for the grace of God, it isn't.

My Personal Grace Story

So many times, we read or hear about stories that have impacted someone else. I want to share a personal testimony of how God continues to bring forth modern-day miracles.

As a senior pastor for almost twenty-five years now, I've had the opportunity to share faith, train others to trust in God, and see God heal people we've prayed for—time and time again. Well, the event I wish to share is a recent incident when God used his people and church to help encourage and lift up another member of the church. It's personal because it is one of my granddaughter's miracle story.

On July 22, 2013, Kaiya was born twelve weeks premature at UCSD Medical Center in San Diego, weighing a mere one pound and eight ounces and measuring just twelve inches long. So not only was she early, but she was also quite underdeveloped and needed life support and incubation for survival, primarily for her lungs. Her Mother had to travel nearly eighty miles eight to ten times a week, creating quite a substantial financial burden.

To make a long story short, she was released from Rady Children's

Hospital in San Diego after a relatively short stay and remarkable improvement in her breathing. With much prayer and medication, her lungs were fully healed to 100 percent capacity. On June 16, she was released, now weighing fifteen pounds and three ounces, and measuring twenty-four inches long. She spent her first Sunday in church on June 22, 2014, with the congregation praising God for answering the prayers we sent up corporately. Now 8 years later, with tambourine in hand, Kaiya has been designated by God as our church's Junior Praise Leader and you better believe, she truly knows God personally!

Kaiya is just one of many miracles I've witnessed God perform in our midst. Our Church Mother is celebrating being cancer-free because of God. Several others have had God remove various illnesses from their bodies. We truly serve a living Savior whose presence and healing touch is alive at New Birth. A young man attacked and stabbed multiple times, left for dead, walked back down the aisle of the church only a couple of weeks later, praising God for protection and healing. There have been others unable to walk who were given strength in their limbs to walk again. Finances, jobs, health, new homes, former substance abusers… God truly is listening to our prayers, and He is ready to open your doors too! Trusting in God means walking boldly as a living testimony of His wonder-working power.

With God on our side, we can overcome any affliction or problem in our lives. All it takes is hope and trust in God that He is a way maker. When your book comes to an end, how will the final chapter read?

Let it speak of how you had some good days and then you also had some bad days. But through it all, God kept you another day to see better times ahead. In Christ, the best is yet to come. Make up your mind today that you will give your life to Christ while you still have breath in your body. So, you messed up! ALL have sinned and fallen short of His Glory, but He still gives us another chance to be "Overcomers." My favorite Gospel song is "Victory Is Mine! Victory Today Is Mine." Join me and the Angels in singing it.

It's all up to you now! Today can be the best new day of your life!